Alfred's Singer's Library of Musical Theatre

TENOR · VOLUME 2

35 SONGS FROM STAGE & FILM

A treasury of songs from stage and film in their original keys, selected by vocal range. Authentic arrangements transcribed from original vocal scores, with authoritative historical and contextual commentary, audition tips, and 16-bar cut suggestions.

EDITED AND COMPILED BY
JOHN L. HAAG AND JEREMY MANN

INTRODUCTION BY BARBARA IRVINE

PLOT SYNOPSES AND COMMENTARY BY
JOHN L. HAAG AND JEREMY MANN

Alfred Publishing Co., Inc.
16320 Roscoe Blvd., Suite 100
P.O. Box 10003
Van Nuys, CA 91410-0003
alfred.com

Copyright © MMVII by Alfred Publishing Co., Inc.
All rights reserved. Printed in USA.

ISBN-10: 0-7390-4970-4
ISBN-13: 978-0-7390-4970-9

Cover Photos
Curtains: © iStockphoto.com / tobkatrina • Manhattan skyline: © iStockphoto.com / BRANDONJ74

Contents

Song Title	Show	Page
A New Town Is A Blue Town	*The Pajama Game*	166
Alone In The Universe	*Seussical the Musical*	188
And They're Off	*A New Brain*	146
The Ballad Of Booth (Part III)	*Assassins*	54
Ballad Of The Easy Life	*The Threepenny Opera*	202
Blah, Blah, Blah	*Delicious*	76
Broadway Baby	*Dames at Sea*	68
Calla Lily Lady	*Two Gentlemen of Verona*	205
Dames	*42nd Street*	41
Different	*Honk*	112
Donna	*Hair*	107
Extraordinary	*Pippin*	171
The Gypsy In Me	*Anything Goes (1987 Revival)*	48
I Want To Make Magic	*Fame: The Musical*	98
I'm Falling In Love With Someone	*Naughty Marietta*	142
I'm Not That Smart	*The 25th Annual Putnam County Spelling Bee*	26
If I Only Had A Brain	*The Wizard of Oz*	218

Song Title	Show	Page
Knowing Me, Knowing You	Mamma Mia	123
Larger Than Life	My Favorite Year	135
Love's Revenge	Two Gentlemen of Verona	210
Lucky To Be Me	On the Town	161
My Unfortunate Erection	The 25th Annual Putnam County Spelling Bee	33
The Phone Call	Lucky Stiff	117
Radames' Letter	Elton John and Tim Rice's "Aida"	45
Sandy	Grease—The Film Version	103
Something To Live For	Sophisticated Ladies	193
Stouthearted Men	The New Moon	155
Strike Up the Band	Stirke Up the Band	198
There's A Boat Dat's Leavin' Soon For New York	Porgy and Bess®	178
They Won't Know Me	Wish You Were Here	214
To Each His Dulcinea	The Man of La Mancha	131
What Am I Doin'?	Closer Than Ever	59
When The Earth Stopped Turning	Elegies	80
You Gotta Die Sometime	Falsettos	89
You Took Advantage Of Me	Present Arms	183

Introduction

Within the opening pages, you will find a synopsis of the plot, the context of the song in each show, the name of the cast member who sang the song in the original production, song type, suggested 16-bar cuts, as well as the standard information such as the show creators, and the dates and theaters of the New York runs. The vocal range for each song can be found in the table of contents. Below are some helpful hints for the singing actor.

Choosing a Song for an Audition

When choosing a song to sing for an audition, ask yourself the following:

1. *Would I ever play the role of the character singing this song?* If not, but you want to sing the song anyway, find a way to make it your own; create your own context after being fully informed about the original context.

2. *Does this song show off my vocal range?* Use the vocal ranges in the table of contents to quickly identify the highest and lowest notes in each song and to determine if they are notes you can sing comfortably.

3. *Is this song appropriate for the show for which I am auditioning?* Use the dates of the first run of each show to determine its era, then compare the era of the song to the era of the show for which you are auditioning; songs from the same era are often similar in style. But, also remember that some later composers write in the style of a previous era or write in various styles. Therefore, if you listen to a recording of the show for which you are auditioning and then listen to the songs you might choose, you can determine if the styles are similar. Singing a song from another show by the same composer who wrote the show for which you are auditioning, can be an even better way to go. If the character who sings your audition song is similar to the character for which you are auditioning, that will help the people on the other side of the table better imagine you in the role. Also, be sure that the song type complies with what is requested in the audition notice.

4. *How do I know if this song is the right type?* Audition notices often ask for a ballad, an uptempo number, a patter song, a comedy number, standard Broadway, legit musical theatre, etc. We have suggested song-type categories for each song. Though a single song may often fall into more than one category, our type categories will serve as a helpful guide.

5. *The audition notice asks for 16 bars; which 16 bars should I sing?* There are many possibilities within each song for usable 16-bar sections. We have suggested one or two possibilities for each song that make some sense in terms of the music and the lyrics, and will show range. But, remember to always learn the entire song; you may be asked to go back and sing all of it after singing your 16 bars.

Have fun at your audition! The time is yours; own it.

The Bottom Line

There is no substitute for a good vocal coach. Go to him or her with your ideas based on the above suggestions, and he or she can then hone in on what will be best for you.

—Barbara Irvine

Barbara Irvine lived in New York City for 15 years, working as a music director/vocal coach/pianist/music copyist/arranger/transcriber/transposer. She has worked with nearly all the major Broadway composers of her time there, as well as with many of the Broadway stars.

Notes

Warning: the paragraphs about the shows may contain plot spoilers.

Any actor mentioned as having originally played a role is from the opening-night cast, unless otherwise indicated.

Some of the suggested 16-bar cuts are slightly longer or shorter than exactly 16 bars in order to create complete sections. Most often, these cuttings will still be accepted at auditions asking for 16 bars. You might choose to use a bar or two preceding the cut as an introduction, or simply ask the audition pianist for a "bell tone" to use as your starting pitch; the latter is more customary and time saving. Bar numbers are indicated as m. #, e. g. bar 16 is indicated as m. 16.

The 25th Annual Putnam County Spelling Bee

The Show

Centering on a fictional spelling bee somewhere in Putnam County, USA, this show follows the inner and outer travails of six eccentric young adolescents as they fiercely compete against each other—with valuable and (and often not-so-valuable) help from parents and other grown-ups around them. The bee's hostess, Rona Lisa Peretti, is a former spelling champion, and the proceedings include a "comfort counselor" for losers, audience volunteers for early rounds of spelling, and a boy contestant who spells out the letters to words with his "magic foot" before speaking them aloud. The musical is based on "C-R-E-P-U-S-C-L-E," a play by Rebecca Feldman.

The Authors

Music and Lyrics by William Finn; Book by Rachel Sheinkin.

New York Runs

May 2, 2005–Present. The role of Leaf Coneybear was originated by Jesse Tyler Ferguson; the role of Chip Tolentino was originated by Jose Llana.

The Song

"I'm Not That Smart"

Leaf Coneybear, a home-schooled boy who sees himself as an underdog in the spelling bee, steps up to the microphone and is given a word to spell. Before doing so, he reveals his inner thoughts to the audience in "I'm Not That Smart." He interrupts himself to spell the word ("acouchi") correctly, and finishes the song triumphantly. Note: in the original production, Leaf occasionally pulled out a finger puppet and expressed through it in a "monster voice."

Song type
Contemporary Musical Theater Comic Uptempo (Youthful)

Suggested 16-bar Audition Cut
m. 47 (including pick-ups) to the end (m. 65). This equals 19 bars; up to 20 bars is generally acceptable for a 16-bar audition.

"My Unfortunate Erection (Chip's Lament)"

Chip Tolentino, last year's Putnam Bee champion, finds himself distracted by the presence of Leaf Coneybear's sister in the audience while trying to spell. He loses his concentration and backtracks to correct a mistake in his spelling, but it is too late. He is eliminated, and soon finds himself relegated to selling snacks at the PTA bake sale. Humiliated and enraged, he sings the lament, "My Unfortunate Erection."

Song type
Contemporary Musical Theater Comic Uptempo (Youthful)

Suggested 16-bar Audition Cut
m. 58 through m. 72; have the accompanist play and sustain the downbeat chord of m. 72 with the vocal sustaining the note 'F' on the word "Life!" (You could write in fermatas over the vocal and piano downbeat in this measure). For a more complete cutting, you may be able to get away with m. 76 (including pickups) through the end (m. 99). This is 23 bars (plus a bass sting), which is over the "20-bar limit." However, the song moves quickly and this version would certainly provide a bigger (and higher) ending.

42nd Street

The Show
Inspired by the classic 1933 Warner Brothers movie musical of the same name, *42nd Street* is the story of young Broadway hopeful Peggy Sawyer and her dreams of performing in a Julian Marsh show. Marsh, a megalomaniacal director currently in rehearsal for his latest extravaganza "Pretty Lady," takes no notice of Peggy at first. But with the help of leading ingénue Billy Lawlor, dance captain Andy Lee, and some friendly chorines, Peggy is cast in the show and makes a positive impression on the director. Disaster strikes, however, when Peggy accidentally trips during an out-of-town rehearsal and causes troublesome diva star Dorothy Brock to break her ankle; Peggy is fired on the spot by Marsh. Left without a star for his show, Marsh is in a quandary—until the chorus members convince him to put Peggy on in Brock's place. The entire company races to the Philadelphia station to catch Peggy before she boards her train for home, and they ultimately convince her to come back and star in the show. With only two days to learn the part, Peggy is nonetheless a triumph, thanks to her talent, hard work, and some unexpected encouragement from Dorothy Brock. Peggy is a star, and "Pretty Lady" an unqualified success.

The Authors
Music by Harry Warren; Lyrics by Al Dubin; Book by Michael Stewart, Mark Bramble; based on the novel by Bradford Ropes. Additional Lyrics by Johnny Mercer and Mort Dixon.

New York Runs
The original New York run of *42nd Street* ran from 1980 -1989: August 25, 1980–March 29, 1981 at the Winter Garden Theatre; March 30, 1981–April 5, 1987 at the Majestic Theatre; March 7, 1987–January 8, 1989 at the St. James Theatre. The role of Billy Lawlor was originated by Lee Roy Reams. The show's first Broadway revival ran from May 5, 2001–January 2, 2005 at the Ford Center for the Performing Arts; David Elder portrayed Billy Lawlor in this production.

The Song
"Dames"

In the first act, the theater troupe travels to Philadelphia for their out-of-town tryout. On the stage of the Arch Street Theatre, Billy leads the chorus in a dress rehearsal of "Dames"—a grand Ziegfeld Follies-style production number that pays tribute to the fairer sex.

Song Type
Standard Musical Theater/Tin Pan Alley Uptempo

Suggested 16-Bar Cut for Auditions
m. 44 through m. 62; cut the piano accompaniment in m. 62 and m. 63 and use m. 64 to complete the rideout under the vocal. This equals 19 bars; up to 20 bars is generally acceptable for a 16-bar audition.

Elton John and Tim Rice's Aida

The Show
Based on Verdi's oft-performed classic grand Opera set in ancient Egypt, John and Rice's *Aida* is a Pop/Rock version of the same story. Aida is a Nubian princess who is captured by soldiers and brought to Egypt as a slave. Radames, the soldiers' powerful commander, falls in love with her and struggles to choose between this love and his loyalty to the Pharaoh. To complicate matters, Radames is loved by and betrothed to Amneris, the Pharaoh's daughter. Ultimately inspired by Aida's courage and love for her people, Radames aids the Nubians, and he and Aida are sentenced to death by the Pharaoh. Amneris convinces her father to allow her to sentence them to be buried alive in a tomb beneath the sands of Egypt. Once there, Aida and Radames vow to find each other even if they have to search for "a hundred lifetimes." The play ends with the souls of the two lovers re-uniting as a modern-day couple in the Egyptian wing of a contemporary museum.

The Authors Music by Elton John; Lyrics by Tim Rice; Book by Linda Woolverton, Robert Falls and David Henry Hwang. Based on the opera by Giuseppe Verdi.

New York Run
March 23, 2000–September 5, 2004 at the Palace Theatre. The role of Amneris was originated by Sherie Rene' Scott; the role of Radames was originated by Adam Pascal.

The Song
"Radames' Letter"
On the eve of her escape from Egypt, Aida receives "Radames' Letter"; as she reads, she hears the young warrior apologize for his past behavior and confess his love for her.

Song Type
Musical Theater Pop Ballad

Suggested 16-Bar Cut for Auditions
m. 9 (including pick-up) to the end (m. 25); this equals 17 bars, which is acceptable for a 16-bar audition.

Anything Goes (1987 Revival Version)

The Show
Like the hit screwball musical comedy of 1935 on which it is based, this revival of *Anything Goes* takes place on a trans-Atlantic pleasure cruise from New York to England. Young Billy Crocker boards the ship to deliver a passport to his traveling boss, Wall Street banker Elisha Whitney; before the ship departs, Billy learns that his long lost love Hope Harcourt is a also passenger, and soon will be married to English Lord Evelyn Oakleigh. Billy stays on board for the cruise, befriends gangster Moonface Martin and his moll, and is himself mistaken for Public Enemy #1. Meanwhile, evangelist-turned-nightclub-singer Reno Sweeney—at first romantically interested in Billy—falls in love with Lord Evelyn. After many twists and turns, outlandish disguises and further mistaken identities, all find wedded bliss in the arms of the right partner.

The Authors
Music and Lyrics by Cole Porter; Original Book by Guy Bolton, P.G. Wodehouse, Howard Lindsay and Russell Crouse; New Book by Timothy Crouse and John Weidman.

New York Run
October 19, 1987–September 3, 1989 at the Vivian Beaumont Theatre. Anthony Heald originated the role of Lord Evelyn Oakleigh.

The Song
"The Gypsy in Me"
In the second act Lord Evelyn realizes that in spite of his imminent wedding to Hope, he is not in love with her—he is really in love with Reno Sweeney. He boldly reveals his awakening passion to the nightclub chanteuse, and serenades her with the confessional "The Gypsy in Me."

Song Type
Standard Musical Theater Comic Uptempo

Suggested 16-bar Audition Cut
m. 59 (including pick-ups) to the end (m. 74).

Assassins

The Show
Assassins is a theatrical examination of the lives and motives of nine Presidential assassins (and would-be assassins) in America, from John Wilkes Booth to Lee Harvey Oswald and beyond. Beginning in a surreal carnival arcade where the nine characters are encouraged to overcome their problems by shooting a president, Assassins proceeds to weave together their stories into a fantasia on the dark side of the American Dream. The assailants transcend time and space to communicate with each other variously, and in the end join forces to convince Oswald to murder President Kennedy—believing that his act will ensure them a glorified place in history.

The Authors
Music and Lyrics by Stephen Sondheim; Book by John Weidman.

New York Runs
Assassins originally played Off-Broadway, December 18, 1990–February 16, 1991 at Playwrights Horizons, with Patrick Cassidy as the Balladeer. The show was revived on Broadway, April 22–July 18, 2004 at Studio 54; Neil Patrick Harris played the Balladeer/Lee Harvey Oswald in this production.

The Song
"Ballad of Booth (Part III)"
Early in the play, the story of John Wilkes Booth is narrated by a singing Balladeer, who also serves as a foil for the assassin. Booth is seen in the feverish moments leading up to his death, during which he clings to his justifications for killing Lincoln. In the "Ballad of Booth (Part III)," the Balladeer refutes these justifications as Booth lays dying, introducing the theme of futility that underlies much of the play.

Song Type
Contemporary Musical Theater Uptempo in a Traditional American Folk Song style.

Suggested 16-Bar Cut for Auditions
m. 19 through m. 35, cut to m. 39 to finish (cutting out bars 36 through 38). This equals 18 bars; up to 20 bars is generally acceptable for a 16-bar audition.

Closer Than Ever

The Show
Like their earlier show *Starting Here, Starting Now*, *Closer Than Ever* is a two-act revue of Maltby and Shire songs, some of which had previously appeared in their book musicals. With humor and poignancy, each song stands alone as a story, exploring adult issues such as getting older, facing mid-life, second marriages, parent-child conflicts and grieving the lost chances of youth.

The Authors
Music by David Shire; Lyrics by Richard Maltby, Jr. Conceived by Steven Scott Smith. "What Am I Doin'?" was originally sung by Brent Barrett for this production.

New York Run
October 17, 1989–July 1, 1990 at the Cherry Lane Theatre.

The Song
"What Am I Doin'?"
In "What Am I Doin'?" a man reminisces about a time in his youth when he behaved crazily because of his obsessive love for a woman. Although he is thankful that he is now older and saner in matters of the heart, he finds himself longing for the craziness of his youth.

Song Type
Contemporary Musical Theater Uptempo

Suggested 16-Bar Cut for Auditions
m. 89 to the end (m. 104). You might be able to get away with m. 83 (including the syncopated "What" at the end of m. 82) to the end; this equals 22 bars, which is above the "20-bar limit" for a 16-bar audition. However, the song moves quickly and this version shouldn't feel too long.

Dames At Sea

The Show
This musical is both an homage to and send-up of 1930's Warner Brothers movie musicals like *42nd Street* and *Dames*. In the story, theatrical producer/manager Hennesy struggles to keep his latest Broadway musical afloat, thanks to difficulties brought about by the Depression and by the show's diva star, Mona Kent. Enter young tap-dancer Ruby, fresh off the bus from Utah and determined to become a Broadway star. She befriends the sassy chorus girl Joan, and falls for Dick, a sailor and aspiring songwriter. Ruby lands a job in the chorus, but Hennesy soon announces that the WPA must tear down the theatre before the show can open. Dick and his sailor buddy Lucky convince their Captain—an old flame of Mona's—to allow the cast to rehearse and perform the musical on board their ship. While rehearsing on deck, Mona becomes violently sea sick; Ruby steps in to replace her at the last minute and becomes a star. In the end, the Captain and Mona, Joan and Lucky, and Ruby and Dick are all married and live happily ever after.

The Authors
Music by Jim Wise; Book and Lyrics by George Haimsohn and Robin Miller.

New York Runs
Off-Broadway, December 20, 1968–May 10, 1970, first at the Bouwerie Lane Theatre, then the Theatre De Lys (now the Lucille Lortel Theatre). David Christmas originated the role of Dick. The show was revived at the Lamb's Theatre in 1985, and again at the Bouwerie Lane Theatre in 2004.

The Song

"Broadway Baby"

Early in the play, Dick and Ruby meet and are instantly smitten with each other. Dick is so inspired by the young chorus girl that he sits down at the piano and begins composing a song about her—"Broadway Baby."

Song Type

Standard Musical Theater Uptempo (1930's homage)

Suggested 16-Bar Cut for Auditions

m. 101 to the end (m. 129); this equals 28 bars in cut time, or the equivalent of 14 bars in 4/4. Another option would be m. 71 through m. 91 (21 bars); have the accompanist sustain the chord on the first beat of m. 91 to finish if using this option.

Delicious

The Show

After six years of success as a writing team for Broadway and Tin Pan Alley, George and Ira Gershwin traveled to California for the first time, to work on the movie musical *Delicious*. The story begins on the S.S. Mauronia, a ship carrying immigrants from Europe to America, and centers on Heather Gordon, a young lady from Scotland. During the voyage, Heather becomes close to a Russian family that includes Sascha, a composer who falls in love with her and begins to write songs for her. She also meets a wealthy first-class passenger named Larry Beaumont, who falls for her as well, in spite of some heat from his girlfriend Diana. The ship eventually arrives at Ellis Island, where Heather is denied entrance to the country due to her uncle's reneging on his promise to support her financially. Nonetheless, she is able to escape the ship and try to make her own way in America—doing her best to avoid the police who pursue her. She manages to keep her romance with Beaumont alive, and joins her Russian friends in their cabaret act.

The Authors

Music by George Gershwin; Lyrics by Ira Gershwin; Screenplay by Guy Bolton and Sonya Levien, from a story by Guy Bolton.

New York Run

Delicious has never been produced as a stage play in New York. In the 1931 film the role of Chris Jansen was played by El Brendel; the role of Olga was played by Manya Roberti.

The Song

"Blah, Blah, Blah"

Much of the comic relief in the film comes from the character Chris Jansen, the Swedish valet of Larry Beaumont. While sailing for America, he serenades fellow passenger Olga with "Blah, Blah, Blah," a song which skewers the clichés of the popular songwriting of the 1920's and '30's.

Song Type

Standard Musical Theater/Tin Pan Alley Standard Comic Uptempo

Suggested 16-Bar Cut for Auditions

m. 41 to the end (m. 56). As the song is in cut time, you might be able to get away with m. 25 to the end (one complete refrain), as this would be the equivalent of 16 bars in 4/4 time.

Elegies: A Song Cycle

The Show

Elegies is a revue of songs written by theater composer William Finn. In each song, Finn pays personal tribute to friends and relatives who have died, from public figures such as Joseph Papp (founder of New York's Public Theater) to his own mother, Barbara. The universal tragedies of the AIDS epidemic and the events of September 11th, 2001 are also addressed. In solos, duets, and trios, a small ensemble expresses Finn's humor, grief, and passion regarding his loved ones—and his ultimate celebration of their unique and colorful lives.

The Author

Music and Lyrics by William Finn.

New York Run

March 2 -30, 2003 at the Mitzi E. Newhouse Theatre. The song "When the Earth Stopped Turning" was sung by Christian Borle in this production.

The Song
"When the Earth Stopped Turning"
In when "When the Earth Stopped Turning," Finn recalls his mother and the life-affirming wisdom she imparted to him, even when facing her own death.

Song Type
Contemporary Musical Theater Ballad

Suggested 16-Bar Cut for Auditions
m. 131 (including pick-ups) to the end (m. 149). This equals 19 bars; up to 20 bars is generally acceptable for a 16-bar audition.

Falsettos

The Show
Falsettos is comprised of two one-act musicals that are part of William Finn's "Marvin Trilogy"—three sung-through plays focusing on Marvin, his wife Trina, his young son Jason, and his male lover, Whizzer. In Act I (originally *March of the Falsettos*), it is 1979, and Marvin is determined to maintain a "Tight-Knit Family" in spite of the fact that he wishes to live with Whizzer as well as his enraged wife and confused son. He seeks the help of his psychiatrist, Mendel, who makes matters worse by moving in on and becoming involved with Trina. In the end, Marvin loses Trina, Mendel and Whizzer, but is hopeful that his relationship with his son is still viable. In Act II (originally *Falsettoland*), it is 1981, Jason is preparing for his bar mitzvah amidst quarrelling parents, and Whizzer—having gotten back together with Marvin—succumbs to a mysterious new disease, yet to be identified as AIDS. In the end, Jason helps reunite everyone by demanding that his bar mitzvah be held in Whizzer's hospital room.

The Authors
Music and Lyrics by William Finn; Book by William Finn and James Lapine.

New York Run
On Broadway, April 29, 1992–June 27, 1993 at the John Golden Theatre, with Stephen Bogardus as Whizzer. Originally produced off-Broadway as two separate shows, *March of the Falsettos* and *Falsettoland*; both productions featured Stephen Bogardus as Whizzer.

The Song
"You Gotta Die Sometime"
Having learned that his illness is terminal, Whizzer is left alone and bedridden in his hospital room, confronting and contemplating death in "You Gotta Die Sometime."

Song Type
Contemporary Musical Theater Dramatic Uptempo

Suggested 16-Bar Cut for Auditions
m. 145 to the end (m. 180); this is 36 bars in a brisk 3/4, which could be considered the equivalent of 18 bars in a moderate 4/4. If you need a shorter cutting, you could try m. 151 (including pick-ups) to the end.

Fame—the Musical

The Show
Based on the popular musical film of 1980, *Fame—the Musical* follows a group of diverse and talented students attending New York's High School for the Performing Arts in the early 1980's. Characters include Carmen Diaz, a fiery Latina dancer with her eyes on Hollywood; Schlomo Metzenbaum, her shy violinist friend; Nick Piazza, a handsome, serious actor; Serena Katz, an insecure actress in love with Nick; and Tyrone Jackson, a street-wise hip-hop dancer who is illiterate. As the students experience the highs and lows of their life at "P.A.," they confront issues such as racism, literacy, sexuality, drug abuse, identity and perseverance. From audition to graduation, they grow as artists and as human beings, and ultimately look toward the future with hopeful determination.

The Authors
Music by Steve Margoshes; Lyrics by Jacques Levy; Book by Jose Fernandez. Based on the film by Alan Parker.

New York Run
Off-Broadway, November 11, 2003–June 27, 2004 at the Little Shubert Theatre. The official title for this production was *Fame on 42nd Street*. Nicole Leach originated the role of Carmen Diaz in this production; Rick Cornette played Nick Piazza, and Sara Schmidt played Serena Katz.

The Song
"I Want to Make Magic"
Early in the play, Nick and Serena rehearse a scene and talk about their life experiences in acting class. Nick reveals that his primary goal as an actor is to move people emotionally; he sings "I Want to Make Magic."

Song Type
Contemporary Musical Theater Ballad

Suggested 16-Bar Cut for Auditions
m. 46 (including pick-ups) to the end (m. 62, plus the bass sting in m. 63). This equals 17 bars, which is acceptable for a 16-bar audition.

Grease (Film Version)

The Show
Like the long-running Broadway musical on which it is based, the film version of *Grease* takes place at Rydell High School in the late 1950's. It is the beginning of the school year, and greaser gang leader Danny Zuko is surprised that his secret summer love—good girl Sandy Olsson (Dumbrowski in the stage version)—has transferred to Rydell. Sandy is equally surprised to see Danny and hopes to continue their romance, but peer pressures force Danny to alter his behavior and treat her coolly. The couple's attempts to reconcile are continually thwarted, leaving Sandy heartbroken. However, her developing friendship with girl gang The Pink Ladies ultimately leads to a transformation that reunites her with Danny for good.

The Authors
Music and Lyrics by Jim Jacobs and Warren Casey; Film Adaptation by Allan Carr; Screenplay by Bronte Woodard. "Sandy" was written by Louis St. Louis and Scott Simon.

New York Runs
The original Broadway production of *Grease* ran from February 14, 1972–April 13, 1980 at the Eden, Broadhurst, Royale and Majestic Theatres. Barry Bostwick originated the role of Danny Zuko. The song "Sandy" was not in this production. There have been two Broadway revivals: May 11, 1994–January 25, 1998 at the Eugene O'Neill Theatre, with Ricky Paull Golden as Danny; and August 19, 2007–present at the Brooks Atkinson Theatre, with Max Crumm as Danny. "Sandy" is sung in the current revival. The film version starred John Travolta as Danny.

The Song
"Sandy"
Inadvertently separated at the school dance to which he had taken her, Danny takes Sandy to a drive-in movie by way of apology. When Sandy suspects that Danny is trying to get "fresh" with her, she angrily leaves, returning the ring he had given her. Left alone and devastated, Danny sings "Sandy."

Song Type
Contemporary Musical Theater Pop Ballad

Suggested 16-Bar Cut for Auditions
m. 27 to m. 42; have the accompanist sustain beat 3 of m. 42 to finish.

Hair

The Show
Billed "the American Tribal Love-Rock Musical," *Hair* has the distinction of being Broadway's first rock musical. At the time it was produced, it pushed the boundaries of musical theater, and indeed seemed to rebel against all previous notions of musical theater. Its incorporation of profanity and nudity shocked audiences initially; nonetheless, the show was a success and ran for over four years. Though essentially non-linear in plot, *Hair* presents the story of Claude, a Viet Nam War draftee, and his friends Berger—a recent high school drop-out and hippie—and Sheila, an anti-war college student. Other members of their "tribe" include Hud, an African-American hippie; Woof, a gay hippie; and Jeanie, a spiritual hippie who is pregnant. Their parents, the government, war and "the establishment" in general are confronted and protested against, as Claude weighs his draft status and the prospect of going to war.

The Authors
Music by Galt MacDermot; Book and Lyrics by Gerome Ragni and James Rado.

New York Runs
April 29, 1968–July 1, 1972 at the Biltmore Theatre. The role of Claude was originated by James Rado; the role of Berger was originated by Gerome Ragni. The show was revived in 1977 at the Biltmore Theatre, with Randall Easterbrook as Claude and Michael Holt as Berger.

The Song
"Donna"
Early in the play, Berger introduces himself and sings "Donna," in which he unleashes his wild, rebellious and confrontational nature for all to experience. In the original production, Berger was dressed in a loincloth and swung out over the audience on a rope during this number.

Song Type
Contemporary Musical Theater Uptempo (Pop/Rock)

Suggested 16-Bar Cut for Auditions
m. 41 through m. 44, take Coda to the end (m. 78); this is 28 bars in cut time, or the equivalent of 14 bars in 4/4. Another option is m. 33 through m. 44, taking the Coda to the end. This is 36 bars (or 18 bars in 4/4); as the tempo of the song is meant to move quickly, this shouldn't feel too long.

Honk!

The Show
Honk! is a musical adaptation of Hans Christian Andersen's classic children's tale, "The Ugly Duckling." The story concerns Ugly, the newly-hatched son of duck parents Ida and Drake. Ugly's different looks and loud "honk" cause his family and neighbors around the barnyard pond to ostracize him and treat him cruelly. Tempted by a wily villain of a Cat, Ugly is led far away from home; his journey to find his way back is fraught with danger and adventure. With help from his devoted mother and some new friends, Ugly ultimately discovers security and happiness as he grows into a beautiful swan.

The Authors
Music by George Stiles; Book and Lyrics by Anthony Drewe; based on the "The Ugly Duckling" by Hans Christian Andersen.

New York Run
Honk! has not been produced professionally in New York City. It opened in London's West End on December 17, 1999, and won the 2000 Laurence Olivier Award for Best Musical. The role of Ugly was portrayed by Gilz Terera in this production.

The Song
"Different"
Recently hatched along with three "normal-looking" siblings, Ugly soon faces ridicule and condemnation from his family and neighbors. To make matters worse, he is unable to "quack" like the other ducks; he is only able to emit a loud, humiliating "HONK!." Shunned away from a meal of French bread, he is left alone and hungry to contemplate his predicament in "Different."

Song Type
Contemporary Musical Theater Ballad

Suggested 16-Bar Cut for Auditions
m. 33 (including pick-ups) to the end (m. 52); this equals 20 bars, which is generally acceptable for a 16-bar audition.

Lucky Stiff

The Show
Lucky Stiff is a farcical murder mystery musical that centers on a mild-mannered English shoe salesman Harry Witherspoon. Harry learns that he has inherited six million dollars from an American uncle he has never met, and that the only way for him to claim the money is by taking his uncle's corpse to Monte Carlo for one last "vacation." If he fails to do this, the money will instead go to the Brooklyn Universal Dog Home. Harry does indeed take "Uncle"—in a wheelchair, wearing sunglasses—to Monte Carlo, unaware that American optometrist Vinnie DiRuzzio and his mob-connected sister Rita LaPorta are en route to Monte Carlo to try to intercept the money. Thrown into this mix is: Annabelle Glick of the Brooklyn Universal Dog Home, who arrives to fight Harry for the money as well; sexy nightclub chanteuse Dominique du Monaco; and mysterious Italian tour guide Luigi Gaudi. As all parties clamor to obtain the six million dollars, Harry and Annabelle find themselves unexpectedly drawn to each other, and the story ends on a note of romantic possibility.

The Authors
Music by Stephen Flaherty; Book and Lyrics by Lynn Ahrens; based on the novel "The Man Who Broke the Bank at Monte Carlo" by Michael Butterworth.

New York Runs
The original production of *Lucky Stiff* opened April 26th, 1988 at Playwrights Horizons, and won the Richard Rodgers Production Award that year. The show was revived at the York Theatre in 2003. Stuart Zagnit played Vinnie in both productions.

The Song
"The Phone Call"
American Rita La Porta, a hard-as-nails woman who is legally blind, confesses to her brother Vinnie that she accidentally murdered her lover while not wearing her glasses. She and the lover had embezzled six million dollars from her mobster husband, and now the money is en route to Monte Carlo, intended as an inheritance for her lover's English nephew—Harry Witherspoon. To make matters worse, Rita confesses that she has blamed the embezzlement on Vinnie, and that the mob is now out to kill him. The siblings must travel to Monte Carlo immediately to retrieve the money. Having arrived at the airport in Nice, a terrified Vinnie calls his wife at home in Atlantic City to try to explain why he's left America and all that's happened to him in "The Phone Call."

Song Type
Contemporary Musical Theater Comic Uptempo

Suggested 16-Bar Cut for Auditions
m. 63 (including pick-ups) to the end (m. 80). This equals 18 bars; up to 20 bars is generally acceptable for a 16-bar audition.

Mamma Mia!

The Show
Featuring songs by the '70's Swedish supergroup ABBA, *Mamma Mia!* tells the story of Donna, a middle-aged English woman who runs a taverna on a fictional Greek island. Donna's live-in daughter Sophie is about to be married and longs to know the identity of the father she's never met, but Donna refuses to talk about him. When Sophie discovers an old diary of her mother's in which three boyfriends are mentioned, she is convinced that one of them must be her father, and invites all three men to her wedding. The men—Harry Bright, a British banker, Bill Austin, an Australian world traveler, and Sam Carmichael, an American architect—all arrive on the island, as do two of Donna's old girlfriends, Tanya and Rosie. As the wedding approaches, Donna must confront her past, and the fact that in spite of lingering bitter feelings between them, she and Sam are still in love. The mystery of Sophie's paternity is never solved, but she grows to love all three men as fathers, and realizes that she must take time to get to know her fiancé Sky better before they marry. Nonetheless, a wedding does take place—between Donna and Sam—and a hopeful Sky and Sophie leave the island to travel the world together.

The Authors
Music and Lyrics by Benny Andersson and Bjorn Ulvaeus; Book by Catherine Johnson; some songs with Stig Anderson; Additional Material by Martin Koch.

New York Run
October 18, 2001–present at the Winter Garden Theatre, with David W. Keeley as Sam Carmichael.

The Song
"Knowing Me, Knowing You"
Sophie, still angry about a fight she's had with Sky, encounters Sam on the beach. Sam talks to Sophie and asks her to think seriously about whether or not she really wants to get married. He recalls the unhappiness of his first marriage in "Knowing Me, Knowing You."

Song Type
Pop Ballad (Contemporary Musical Theater)

Suggested 16-Bar Cut for Auditions
m. 81 to the end (m. 100); this is 20 bars, which is generally acceptable for a 16-bar audition. You could also cut bars 93 to 96 if you need a shorter version.

Man Of La Mancha

The Show
Based on Cervantes' classic epic novel *Don Quixote, Man of La Mancha* is actually a play within a play: In a bleak prison dungeon in sixteenth century Spain, the author Cervantes is introduced as a man imprisoned for failing to pay taxes. Told that he must be tried by his fellow prisoners and surrender his possessions to them if found guilty, Cervantes produces a trunk full of theatrical props, and proceeds with his "defense": an acting out of the story of "knight-errant" Don Quixote de la Mancha and his adventures with his squire Sancho Panza; as the story proceeds, the prisoner audience is employed to play various characters in the story. From the beginning, it appears that Don Quixote is insane: he fights a windmill as if it was a dragon, and treats tavern servant Aldonza—a woman most consider to be the lowest of prostitutes—as though she was "Dulcinea," a fair lady of the highest rank. Soon it is learned that "Don Quixote" is in reality a country gentlemen named Alonso Quixana, whose family and priest are alarmed and ashamed by his scandalous behavior; his niece's cruel fiancé Dr. Carrasco ultimately conspires to strip him of his delusions. But to the end, Quixote fights valiantly for his chivalrous ideals in the face of a harsh and bitter world, and his power to transform lives for the better is assured. *Man of La Mancha* ends with Cervantes being led away from the dungeon by officers of the Inquisition, as the other prisoners sing Quixote's idealistic anthem "The Impossible Dream."

The Authors
Music by Mitch Leigh; Lyrics by Joe Darion; Book by Dale Wasserman. Suggested by the life and works of Miguel de Cervantes y Saavedra.

New York Runs
The original production of *Man of La Mancha* ran Off-Broadway from November 22, 1965–March 18, 1968 at the ANTA Washington Square Theatre; Robert Rounseville originated the role of the Padre. The show transferred to Broadway and ran March 20, 1968–March 1, 1971 at the Martin Beck Theatre; March 3–May 24, 1971 at the Eden Theatre; and May 26–June 26, 1971 at the Mark Hellinger Theatre. The show has had four Broadway revivals, most recently December 5, 2002–August 31, 2003 at the Martin Beck Theatre, with Marc Jacoby as the Padre.

The Song
"To Each His Dulcinea"
The family priest, known as the Padre, learns that Dr. Carrasco is determined to effect a "cure" that will rid Alonso Quixana of the delusion that he is Don Quixote. Left alone, the Padre sings "To Each His Dulcinea," in which dreams about a world in which every man has the inspiration that Quixote finds in his Dulcinea.

Song Type
Contemporary Musical Theater Ballad

Suggested 16-Bar Cut for Auditions
m. 41 (including pick-up) to the end (m. 74). This is 34 bars in a "Lively" 3/4, which is could be considered the equivalent of 17 bars in a moderate 4/4. If necessary, you could cut m. 67 through m. 70 to create a shorter rideout under the vocal.

My Favorite Year

The Show
Set in New York City in 1954, *My Favorite Year* is the story of young Benjy Stone, a freshman writer for the hit television show The King Kaiser Comedy Cavalcade. When aging movie star Alan Swann, a hard-drinking Errol Flynn type, is set to guest star on the program, Benjy is thrilled about the prospect of meeting his childhood movie hero. But soon a very inebriated Swann arrives at the writers' office and passes out, and King Kaiser threatens to replace him on the show. Benjy begs Kaiser to reconsider, and Kaiser agrees to let Swann stay—on the condition that Benjy act as his chaperone for the week of rehearsals leading up to the show's live broadcast. If Benjy fails to keep Swann sober and out of trouble, he will lose his job writing for Kaiser. As the week proceeds, Benjy manages to keep Swann in line; he even takes him to dinner at his family's home in Brooklyn, and all goes well…until Swann learns that his estranged daughter Tess is in town and wants to see him. When Tess shows up in the audience at the live broadcast, Swann is unable to go onstage, and it looks like the show will be a disaster. But at the last minute, Swann follows through to save the show and reunite with his

daughter—and Benjy learns some lessons about real-life courage and heroism.

The Authors
Music by Stephen Flaherty; Lyrics by Lynn Ahrens; Book by Joseph Dougherty; based on the motion picture "My Favorite Year" by Dennis Palumbo and Norman Steinberg.

New York Run
December 10, 1992–January 10, 1993 at the Vivian Beaumont Theatre. The role of Benjy Stone was originated by Evan Pappas.

The Song
"Larger Than Life"

When Benjy learns that Alan Swann is to guest star on the King Kaiser show, his excitement turns into poignant nostalgia, as he reminisces about his childhood in "Larger Than Life."

Song Type
Contemporary Musical Theater Ballad

Suggested 16-Bar Cutting for Auditions
m. 85 to the end (m. 105); this is 21 bars, which is slightly longer than the "20 bar limit" for a 16-bar audition. You could cut the piano accompaniment in m. 101 through m. 104 to condense the rideout; this cutting would equal 18 bars.

Naughty Marietta

The Show
Set in New Orleans in 1780, *Naughty Marietta* concerns American Captain Richard Warrington and his mission to capture a notorious French pirate named Bras-Pique. Soon after he arrives in the city, Warrington meets and befriends the mischievous Marietta, a young runaway Italian countess. Though the two are attracted to each other romantically, Warrington is determined to stay focused on his search for Bras-Pique and tells Marietta he has no time for love. Marietta is in turn pursued as a wife by the strong-willed Lieutenant Governor's son, Etienne Grandet. After misunderstanding

Warrington's intentions regarding another woman, an angry Marietta consents to marry Grandet—a marriage that is prevented in the nick of time by the revelation that Grandet is in reality the pirate Bras-Pique. The villain manages to escape, and Warrington and Marietta are united in love.

The Authors
Music by Victor Herbert; Book and Lyrics by Rida Johnson Young

New York Runs
November 11, 1910–March 4, 1911 at the New York Theatre. The role of Captain Richard Warrington was originated by Orville Harrold. The operetta was revived twice on Broadway, in 1929 at Jolson's 59th Street Theatre and in 1931 at Erlanger's Theatre; both productions featured Roy Cropper as Captain Richard. *Naughty Marietta* was subsequently produced as a film in 1935, starring Jeanette MacDonald and Nelson Eddy.

The Song
"I'm Falling in Love With Someone"

At an elite masked ball, Marietta decides to marry Etienne Grandet in order to spite Captain Richard. Realizing that his feelings for Marietta have become quite serious, the heretofore stoic Captain expresses the disconcerting emotions he is experiencing in "I'm Falling in Love With Someone."

Song Type
Legit/Operetta Ballad

Suggested 16-Bar Cut for Auditions
m. 53 (including pick-ups) to the end (m. 68).

A New Brain

The Show
A New Brain is William Finn's semi-autobiographical account of a songwriter who is suddenly stricken with a serious (and possibly terminal) brain condition. At the beginning of the play, Gordon Schwinn is struggling to write a song for his boss Mr. Bungee, the tyrannical frog-host of a children's television program. At lunch with his friend Rhoda, Gordon complains about not being able to do the writing he really wants to do; after

Mr. Bungee appears to him as a hallucination, Gordon collapses face-first into his pasta. He is rushed to the hospital, where he is diagnosed with a rare brain condition that requires surgery. With his loved ones around him (Rhoda, his mother, and his partner, Roger), Gordon faces his mortality—and the terrifying prospect that he has "so many songs" within him that may never be written. What follows is a nightmarish and often comic odyssey in which Gordon manages to create songs in spite of his condition: in his hospital bed, while in an MRI chamber, and even while in a coma. The songs weave together bits of his past, his present, and his imagined future, all featuring a host of characters both intimate and remote to him. His imagination, creativity and sense of humor prevail and indeed seem to pull him through; in the end he survives his operation and recovers, with a renewed sense of freedom and a new perspective on his life and relationships.

The Authors
Music and Lyrics by William Finn; Book by James Lapine. The vocal arrangements were created by Jason Robert Brown.

New York Run
June 18–August 23, 1998 at the Mitzi E. Newhouse Theatre. Malcolm Gets originated the role of Gordon.

The Song
"And They're Off"
Newly arrived in the hospital and unsure of his prognosis, Gordon reflects on his estranged father's history of addictive gambling and its destructive effect on the family in "And They're Off." In the play, several members of the ensemble provide back-up vocals and story-telling during the song.

Song Type
Contemporary Musical Theater Uptempo (Pop)

Suggested 16-Bar Cut for Auditions:
m. 126 (including pick-ups) to the end (m. 140). You could also try m. 117 (from the shouted "And they're off!") to the end; this equals 24 bars, which might be pushing it—but the song moves quickly and this cutting would feel more complete.

The New Moon

The Show
Based on the real-life adventures of a French aristocrat turned revolutionary, *The New Moon* begins in New Orleans in 1792. Robert Mission, a young political refugee from France, is hiding his true identity by living as a bond-servant to wealthy ship owner Monsieur Beaunoir. Robert falls in love with Beaunoir's beautiful daughter Marianne, and the girl responds in kind. However, Robert believes she has betrayed him when he is caught by Vicomte Ribaud, a French Royalist detective dispatched to return him to France to be put on trial. Robert is taken to the ship The New Moon, and Marianne steals aboard to be with him, ultimately convincing him of her love. As the ship is sailing for France, Robert instigates a mutiny, and he and the crew seize power. They land at the Isle of Pines, where a new free republic is established. Ribaud tries to lead a revolt against Robert and his men, and is encouraged when French ships arrive at the island. But the news from France is not in Ribaud's favor: the Republican Revolution has succeeded there, and all aristocrats must renounce their titles or face the guillotine. Ribaud is taken back to France to be executed, but Robert renounces his title, and his new island republic flourishes—as does the romance between Robert and Marianne.

The Authors
Music by Sigmund Romberg; Lyrics by Oscar Hammerstein II; Book by Oscar Hammerstein II, Frank Mandel and Laurence Schwab.

New York Runs
September 19, 1928–December 14, 1929 at the Imperial and Casino Theatres, with Robert Halliday as Robert Mission and William O'Neal as Phillipe. The show was revived in 1944 at City Center, with Earl Wrightson as Robert and John Hamill as Phillipe.

The Song
"Stout-Hearted Men"
In the first act, the song "Stout-Hearted Men" is led by Robert and Phillipe in New Orleans' Café Creole, to help rally their French compatriots to

the revolutionary cause. In the play, the number evolves into a choral song for the male ensemble.

Song Type
Legit/Operetta Uptempo.

Suggested 16-Bar Cut for Auditions
m. 54 to the end (m. 77). This is 16 bars in 2/4 time, or the equivalent of 8 bars in 4/4. Another option would be m. 58 (including pick-up) to the end, which would add four 4/4 bars to the first option (or the equivalent of 12 bars total).

On The Town

The Show
Inspired by Jerome Robbins' ballet *Fancy Free* (also with music by Leonard Bernstein), *On the Town* is the story of three young sailors on leave for 24 hours in New York City during World War II. As they set out to experience as much fun and adventure as they can, they all find romance: Gabey becomes infatuated with the lovely but elusive Ivy Smith, this month's "Miss Turnstiles" of the subway; Ozzie clicks with the beautiful anthropologist Claire de Loone at the natural history museum; and Chip is swept off his feet by sassy lady cab driver Hildy Esterhazy. Although they all wish to spend time together, Ivy is for various reasons unable to meet with Gabey for any length of time. He searches for her through an odyssey of night club episodes with the others, and eventually finds her dancing at Coney Island in the wee hours of the morning. By this time, the wild adventures of the young sailors catch up with them and they are arrested. They are escorted back to their ship in time for departure and are delighted as, at the last instant, Ivy, Claire and Hildy arrive at the dock to bid them a fond goodbye. The boys ship off, and a new trio of sailors arrives—joyfully preparing for their 24 hours on the town.

The Authors
Music by Leonard Bernstein; Lyrics and Book by Betty Comden and Adolph Green based on an idea by Jerome Robbins.

New York Runs December 28, 1944–June 2, 1945 at the Adelphi Theatre; June 4–July 28, 1945 at the 44th Street Theatre; and July 30, 1945–February 2, 1946 at the Martin Beck Theatre.

John Battles originated the role of Gabey. The show was revived on Broadway in 1971 at the Imperial Theatre, with Ron Hussman, and again in 1998 at the George Gershwin Theatre, with Perry Laylon Ojeda as Gabey.

The Song
"Lucky to be Me"
After falling in love with her "Miss Turnstiles" picture in the subway, Gabey manages to find Ivy Smith at her singing lesson in Carnegie Hall. The two are smitten with each other, and plan to meet later that evening in Times Square. Gabey appears for the rendezvous at the appointed time, and sings "Lucky to be Me" in anticipation of his date with Ivy.

Song Type
Standard Musical Theater Ballad

Suggested 16-Bar Cut for Auditions
m. 54 to the end (m. 71). This equals 18 bars; up to 20 bars is generally acceptable for a 16-bar audition.

The Pajama Game

The Show
Set in and around the Sleep-Tite Pajama Factory in Cedar Rapids, Iowa, *The Pajama Game* examines what can happen when love infiltrates labor/management relations. New factory superintendent Sid Sorokin finds himself falling for Babe Williams—an attractive woman who also happens to be the head of the union grievance committee. She and the other union workers are demanding a raise of 7½ cents an hour from management; the boss, Mr. Hasler, will not budge, and Sid toes the management line along with him. As the romance between Sid and Babe heats up, labor tensions increase. The workers stage a slow-down in production, leading Sid to fire Babe—in spite of the fact that he is sympathetic to her cause. Suspecting that boss Hasler has been doing some shady bookkeeping (and unable to face losing Babe for good), Sid finds a way to view the company's secret financial records. Armed with incriminating evidence, Sid convinces Hasler to meet the union's demands and raise wages by 7½ cents. The workers are happy, and the union of Sid and Babe is assured.

The Authors
Music by Richard Adler and Jerry Ross; Book by George Abbott and Richard Bissell; based on the novel "7½ Cents" by Richard Bissell.

New York Runs
Original run: May 13, 1954–November 10, 1956 at the St. James Theatre and November 12, 1956–November 24, 1956 at the Shubert Theatre. The role of Sid Sorokin was originated by John Raitt. The show has been revived twice on Broadway: December 9, 1973–February 3, 1974 at the Lunt-Fontanne Theatre, with Hal Linden as Sid; and February 23–June 17, 2006 at the American Airlines Theatre, with Harry Connick, Jr. as Sid.

The Song
"A New Town is a Blue Town"
Early in the play, new superintendent Sid Sorokin comes to the factory floor to help fix a broken sewing machine with two employees. As Sid goes to work, the employees complain about their wages instead of helping him. Angered, Sid pushes one of them, causing the employee to leave to file a complaint with the union. Left alone, Sid sings of his determination to overcome the challenges of his new situation, in "A New Town is a Blue Town."

Song Type
Standard Musical Theater Ballad

Suggested 16-Bar Cut for Auditions
m. 47 (including pick-ups) to the end (m. 57), equaling 11 bars. For a longer cutting (and in a lower key): m. 22 (including pick-up) to beat 3 of m. 38; have the accompanist sustain beat 3 of the piano accompaniment in this last bar. This version is 17 bars, which is acceptable for a 16-bar audition.

Pippin

The Show
Pippin is an allegorical pop musical set in medieval France during the reign of Charlemagne. The story is introduced by a traveling theatrical troupe of "Players," led by a Leading Player who both narrates and manipulates the action: young Pippin, the first-born son of Charlemagne, returns home from University and immediately begins to search for his purpose in life. He first tries to find glory in helping fight a war with his father, but is disgusted by the destruction it causes, even in victory. The Leading Player then suggests he pursue a simpler life, so Pippin visits his exiled Grandmother in the country, who advises him to "just live." He takes her advice and pursues an idyllic life of romance, but is soon overwhelmed by women and men who are only interested in sexual relationships. The Leading Player advises him to take a political course and speak out against Charlemagne, which ultimately leads to his assassinating his own father and being crowned the New King. But Pippin soon falters in his rule and— with the help of the increasingly devilish Leading Player—resurrects his father, who restores himself as king. Discouraged that he still hasn't found his purpose, Pippin is reassured by the Leading Player; he soon meets a widow with a small son and tries to live a domestic life with them on her estate. But this, too, fails to satisfy him, and he walks away from his new family. The Players then try to convince him to commit suicide by grand self-immolation as a way of glorifying himself and his legacy. Pippin comes close to following through on this, but stops. The widow and her young son appear, and Pippin joins them. The Leading Player angrily begins stripping the stage of all of its theatrical elements, until the domestic trio is left alone on a bare stage. Pippin seems to have finally found happiness.

The Authors
Music and Lyrics by Stephen Schwartz; Book by Roger O. Hirson and Bob Fosse.

New York Runs
October 23, 1972–March 13, 1977 at the Winter Garden Theatre and March 15, 1977–June 12, 1977 at the Minskoff Theatre. The role of Pippin was originated by John Rubinstein.

The Song
"Extraordinary"
Soon after meeting the widow Catherine and her young son Theo, it seems that the despondent Pippin may have found his new lease on life:

Catherine asks him to help her run her estate. This he does, and begins to help with all the everyday menial chores that must be done. He quickly grows dissatisfied with the work, however, and sings "Extraordinary."

Song Type
Contemporary Musical Theater Uptempo (Pop)

Suggested 16-Bar Cut for Auditions
m. 75 to the end (m. 89), equaling 15 bars. Another option would be m. 4 to m. 19; have the accompanist play a B-flat "sting chord" on beat three of m. 19 to finish, if using this option.

Porgy And Bess®

The Show
Billed as "An American Folk Opera in Three Acts," *Porgy and Bess* is considered by many to be George Gershwin's masterwork, and to this day enjoys revivals in opera houses all over the world. Set in the early 1930's in Catfish Row, a poor section of Charleston, South Carolina, the story begins with a murder: Crown kills Robbins over a dice game, and flees. He leaves behind his girlfriend, Bess, who is in turn pressured by drug pusher Sportin' Life to run away with him to New York. Alone and shunned by all, Bess is comforted in the arms of Porgy, a kind handicapped man who protects her. When a picnic is planned on Kittiwah Island, Porgy encourages Bess to attend; she leaves him in Catfish Row, only to find Crown hiding on the island. Crown persuades her to stay with him, but a week later she returns to Porgy, sick and frightened that Crown will come after her. Porgy promises to protect her. Soon a hurricane approaches the coast, and Crown is injured while attempting to rescue a fisherman. He returns for Bess, but Porgy kills him. Porgy is taken to jail, leaving Bess vulnerable to Sportin' Life, who finally convinces Bess to run away with him to New York. Porgy is released from jail for lack of evidence. The neighbors tell him Bess has left with Sportin' Life, and Porgy sets out for New York to find her.

The Authors
Music by George Gershwin; Lyrics by DuBose Heyward and Ira Gershwin; Libretto by DuBose Heyward, based on the play *Porgy* by DuBose Heyward and Dorothy Heyward.

New York Run
October 10, 1935–January 25, 1936, at the Alvin Theatre. There have been 5 Broadway revivals. John W. Bubbles originated the role of Sportin' Life.

The Song
"There's a Boat Dat's Leavin' Soon for New York"
After Porgy is taken to jail, Bess is left alone with Sportin' Life, who ultimately convinces her to run away with him in "There's a Boat Dat's Leavin' Soon for New York."

Song type
Standard Musical Theater Uptempo/Midtempo with a jazzy feel

Suggested 16-Bar Cut for Auditions
m. 44 (including pick-ups) to the end (m. 59).

Present Arms

The Show
Set in Hawaii, *Present Arms* concerns young Marine Private Chick Evans, a plumber's son from Brooklyn. Wanting to impress the aristocratic young Lady Delphine, Evans poses as a Captain, but is soon caught and dismissed from the service—and from Lady Delphine's attentions. Ultimately, Evans manages to win over the young lady by saving the day when a yacht is shipwrecked, and the two unite in love.

The Authors
Music by Richard Rodgers; Lyrics by Lorenz Hart; Book by Herbert Fields.

New York Runs
April 26–September 1, 1928 at Lew Fields' Mansfield Theatre. The role of Douglas Atwell was originated by Busby Berkeley, who also choreographed the production.

The Song
"You Took Advantage of Me"
Early in the play, Marine Sergeant Douglas Atwell and visiting tourist Edna Stevens express their mutual attraction to each other in "You Took Advantage of Me."

Song Type
Standard Musical Theatre/Tin Pan Alley Standard Uptempo.

Suggested 16-Bar Cut for Auditions
m. 37 to the end (m. 152).

Seussical the Musical

The Show
Seussical the Musical is based on several beloved children's books by Dr. Seuss, primarily *Horton Hears a Who!*. The Cat in the Hat serves as the play's narrator, and occasionally manipulates the action to stir things up. The main story revolves around Horton the Elephant; he is determined to save the people of Whoville, a town that exists on a tiny speck of dust perched upon a piece of clover. Only Horton can hear the cries of the Whos, and his friends and neighbors ridicule him for speaking to and trying to protect a seemingly insignificant dust speck. One of his neighbors—the bird Gertrude McFuzz—believes in Horton's cause, and wants to help him. Unfortunately, Horton fails to notice her, which she attributes to her meager one-feather tail. As the play proceeds, other Dr. Seuss characters and stories are woven into the action, and in the end, Whoville and its inhabitants are saved, Gertrude is noticed, and Horton hatches an Elephant Bird!

The Authors
Music by Stephen Flaherty; Lyrics by Lynn Ahrens; Book by Lynn Ahrens and Stephen Flaherty; Conceived by Ahrens, Flaherty and Eric Idle. Based on the works of Dr. Seuss.

New York Run
November 30, 2000–May 20, 2001 at the Richard Rodgers Theatre. The role of Gertrude McFuzz was originated by Janine LaManna; the role of Horton was originated by Kevin Chamberlin.

The Song
"Alone in the Universe"
Horton the Elephant, ostracized for guarding the speck of dust that supports the tiny town of Whoville, sings "Alone in the Universe"—affirming his new-found purpose and determination to protect the Whos. In the play, he is joined in song by JoJo, a young boy in Whoville who has been sent to military school because of his lively imagination.

Song Type
Contemporary Musical Theater Ballad (Pop)

Suggested 16-Bar Cut for Auditions
m. 21 (including pick-up) through m. 39; have the accompanist sustain an F chord under the vocal in m. 39. Another option would be m49 (including pick-up) through m. 67; the accompanist can play m. 73 (the last measure of the song) as the rideout for the vocal in m. 67. Both of these options are 19 bars long; up to 20 bars is generally acceptable for a 16-bar audition.

Sophisticated Ladies

The Show
Sophisticated Ladies is a musical revue that celebrates the music of American jazz composer and bandleader Duke Ellington. Set within a grand nightclub atmosphere that evokes Harlem's Cotton Club of the 1920's and '30's, the show features over two dozen of Ellington's great standards, including "In a Sentimental Mood," "I'm Beginning to See the Light," and "It Don't Mean a Thing (If It Ain't Got That Swing)." Larger-than-life characters sing and dance to a live onstage big band, expressing the unique exuberance, romance and sophistication of Ellington's compositions.

The Authors
Conceived by Donald McKayle, based on the music of Duke Ellington. "Something to Live For" was written by Duke Ellington and Billy Strayhorn.

New York Run
March 1, 1981–January 2, 1983 at the Lunt-Fontanne Theatre. "Something to Live For" was sung by Gregory Hines in this production.

The Song
"Something to Live For"
1939's "Something to Live For" is a poignant jazz ballad in which a wealthy man expresses his deep yearning for one thing that money can't buy: true love.

Song Type
Tin Pan Alley Standard/Jazz Standard Ballad

Suggested 16-Bar Cut for Auditions
m. 60 to the end (m. 80). This equals 21 bars, which is slightly longer than the "21-bar limit." You could eliminate m. 79 in the piano accompaniment to reduce the cutting to 20 bars.

Strike Up The Band

The Show
Notable as the first of the Gershwin's musical political satires, Strike Up the Band was originally produced in 1927, but closed during its out of town tryout in Philadelphia due to poor audience attendance. It was re-vamped significantly in 1930, with its satirical edge softened by playwright Morrie Ryskind, and was a success on Broadway. Today, the 1927 version is considered by many to be superior, and—as this is the only version currently available for production—its plot is summarized here: Horace J. Fletcher, the wealthy owner of the Fletcher American Cheese Company, is incensed when Switzerland imposes a 50% tariff on imported cheese. As a mogul with clout in Washington, D.C., Fletcher convinces the U.S. government to declare war on Switzerland—a war he finances himself as "The Horace J. Fletcher Memorial War." Newspaper reporter Jim Townsend criticizes the war and the fact that Fletcher has been using Grade B milk in his cheese, outraging Fletcher. The situation is made worse when Fletcher's daughter Joan confesses her love for Townsend. In retaliation, Fletcher has Townsend drafted and sent to fight in Switzerland; once there, it becomes clear that that the war is a travesty (for example, the American soldiers spend all their time knitting in deluxe hotel accommodations, and no one can seem to find the "enemy"). Nonetheless, Townsend manages to help win the war, go home as a hero, and marry Joan. The play ends with the announcement that Russia is incensed by an American tariff on caviar, and once again the Americans are inspired to fight a new war.

The Authors
Music by George Gershwin; Lyrics by Ira Gershwin; Book by Morrie Ryskind, based on a libretto by George S. Kaufman.

New York Run
January 14–June 28, 1930 at the Times Square Theatre. The role of Jim Townsend was originated by Jerry Goff.

The Song
"Strike up the Band"
Toward the end of Act I, reporter Jim Townsend—already deemed unpatriotic for criticizing the war—is found to be wearing a Swiss watch, and is thus arrested for being a spy. He is tried by the Very Patriotic League—led by Horace J. Fletcher—and is sentenced to fight in Switzerland. Soon a parade of American troops enters, Jim joins them, and they all march off to war singing "Strike up the Band."

Song Type
Standard Musical Theater/Tin Pan Alley Standard Uptempo

Suggested 16-Bar Cut for Auditions
m. 47 (including pick-ups) to the end (m. 62). Another option would be m. 31 (including pick-ups) to the end. This is 32 bars in cut time, or the equivalent of 16 bars in 4/4, which shouldn't feel too long.

The Threepenny Opera

The Show
Based on John Gay's 18th century English ballad opera, *The Beggar's Opera*, Brecht and Weill's *Threepenny Opera* is a landmark work of socio-political musical theater. Set in the seedy underworld of Victorian London, the story centers around Macheath (Mackie Messer, or Mack the Knife), a vicious criminal "anti-hero." Macheath marries Polly Peachum, the daughter of Jonathan Jeremiah Peachum, boss of London's beggars. Infuriated by the union, Peachum tries to have Macheath executed, but is thwarted by chief of police Tiger Brown, a childhood friend of the criminal. Nonetheless, Peachum eventually manages to get Macheath arrested and sentenced to hang. Moments before the execution, however, Macheath is pardoned by the Queen and granted a castle and a pension.

The Authors
Music by Kurt Weill, Book and German Lyrics by Bertolt Brecht; English adaptation of Book and Lyrics by Marc Blitzstein.

New York Runs
The first American version was produced on Broadway, running from April 13-22, 1933 at the Empire Theatre, with Robert Chisholm as Macheath. It was revived Off-Broadway at the Theater de Lys, first running from March 10–May 30, 1954, then from September 20, 1955–December 17, 1961. Scott Merrill portrayed Macheath in this revival. The show has had three major New York revivals, most recently in 2006, with Alan Cumming as Macheath.

The Song
"Ballad of the Easy Life"
In the second act, Macheath is persuaded by Polly that her father will indeed have him arrested. He decides to leave London, but not before visiting his ex-lover Jenny in the brothel where she is employed. Unbeknownst to him, Jenny has been bribed by Mrs. Peachum to turn him in, and he is soon hauled away to jail by Tiger Brown. Once in jail, Macheath sings "Ballad of the Easy Life," in which he affirms that an abundance of money does in fact make for a better life.

Song Type
Brecht/Weill Uptempo/Midtempo

Suggested 16-Bar Cut for Auditions
m. 5 (including pick-up), to the end (m. 25, taking the second ending), choosing the verse you prefer. This equals 20 bars, which is generally acceptable for a 16-bar audition.

Two Gentlemen Of Verona

The Show
A rock musical based on Shakespeare's comedy of youthful love and betrayal, *Two Gentlemen of Verona* focuses on Valentine and Proteus, best friends who leave their hometown of rural Verona for the big city of Milan. There, Valentine falls in love with the Duke's daughter Silvia, who has been promised to the wealthy but doltish Thurio. Valentine schemes to steal Silvia away (with her consent), but his efforts are thwarted by his old friend Proteus, who has fallen for her as well—and who has abandoned his pregnant sweetheart Julia back in Verona. Proteus plans to betray Valentine by telling the Duke of his plot to kidnap his daughter. Meanwhile, the spurned Julia and her maidservant travel to Milan dressed as men in order to find Proteus and confront him. Because the musical was originally written for the New York Shakespeare Festival's Central Park performances, and toured New York City neighborhoods in 1971, the score was written to reflect the wide variety of ethnic and popular music of that time and place. Thus, there are elements of Latino, Caribbean, and African-American music in the score, as well as rock, pop, doo-wop and R & B.

The Authors
Music by Galt MacDermot; Lyrics by John Guare; Book adapted by John Guare and Mel Shapiro, from the play by William Shakespeare.

New York Run
December 1, 1971–May 20, 1973 at the St. James Theatre. The role of Julia was originated by Diana Davila; the role of Valentine was originated by Clifton Davis; the role of Proteus was originated by Raul Julia. The show was revived in 2005

at the Delacorte Theatre in Central Park, with Rosario Dawson as Julia, Norm Lewis as Valentine and Oscar Isaac as Proteus.

The Songs
"Calla Lily Lady"
At the end of Act I, Proteus decides that he must betray his best friend Valentine in order to move in on Valentine's newfound love, the "celestial" Silvia. Proteus celebrates his decision—and the prospect of being united with Silvia—in "Calla Lily Lady."

Song Type
Contemporary Musical Theater Comic Uptempo (Pop)

Suggested 16-Bar Cut for Auditions
m. 22 (including pick-ups) through the downbeat of m. 37. You could also use the accompaniment of the last bar (m. 71) as the rideout for the vocal in m. 37.

"Love's Revenge"
Valentine, having traveled to the big city of Milan to seek honor and fortune, immediately finds himself in love at the first sight of Silvia, the Duke of Milan's dazzling daughter. He sings about the emotional upheaval he is experiencing in "Love's Revenge."

Song Type
Contemporary Musical Theater Ballad (Pop)

Suggested 16-Bar Cut for Auditions
m. 15 (including pick-ups) to the end (m. 31), which equals 17 bars. Note: as this song was written to be in the style of a soul or R & B number, it is customary to take some liberties with the melody (for example, adding gospel "riffs," etc).

Wish You Were Here

The Show
Taking place at Camp Karefree—a fictional Catskills summer camp for adults—*Wish You Were Here* concerns a soon-to-be-married young woman named Teddy Sterns. Advised by her doctor to relax before her wedding, Teddy travels from Manhattan to Camp Karefree for a two-week vacation. Within a few days, she finds herself romantically entangled with two of the young men on the camp's staff: Pinky Harris, a womanizer who sees her as a sexual trophy; and Chick Miller, a sincere law student who falls in love with her. Teddy falls for Chick as well, but after she tells him she is engaged, the two decide to avoid each other. This creates an opening for Pinky to move in on Teddy, which leads to tensions and misunderstandings that affect the entire camp. At the end of the two weeks, Teddy leaves to return to New York, but—having realized that she no longer wants to marry her fiancé— soon returns to unite with Chick.

The Authors
Music and Lyrics by Harold Rome; Book by Arthur Kober and Joshua Logan, based on the play "Having Wonderful Time" by Arthur Kober.

New York Run
June 25, 1952–November 28, 1953 at the Imperial Theatre. The role of Chick Miller was originated by Jack Cassidy.

The Song
"They Won't Know Me"
After a week at camp together, Chick takes Teddy to a remote romantic spot called Eagle Rock. There, he confesses that he is in love with her, and proposes marriage. Hoping that her answer will be yes, he imagines his subsequent transformation in "They Won't Know Me."

Song Type
Standard Musical Theater Ballad.

Suggested 16-Bar Cut for Auditions
m. 26 (including pick-up) to the end (m. 45). This is 20 bars (or 19, if you count the last two 2/4 bars as one bar of 4/4). Up to 20 bars is generally acceptable for a 16-bar audition. If you need a shorter cutting, you could try m. 34 (including pick-ups) to the end.

The Wizard Of Oz

The Show

Based on the classic MGM movie musical (which was in turn based on the children's book by L. Frank Baum), *The Wizard of Oz* is the story of Dorothy Gale, a young girl living on a Kansas farm with her Aunt Em and Uncle Henry. Facing threats from the evil Miss Gulch, who tries to have her dog Toto destroyed, Dorothy decides to run away. En route, she meets a traveling entertainer named Professor Marvel, who convinces her to go back home. But by the time she gets back, a cyclone has reached the farm, and Dorothy and Toto are swept up in it, inside the farmhouse. The cyclone drops them in the wonderful world of Oz, where Dorothy discovers that her house accidentally landed on and killed a witch—the sister of the Wicked Witch of the West, who now wants revenge (and her sister's magical ruby slippers, which found themselves on Dorothy's feet soon after she landed in Oz). Hoping to find a way back home to Kansas, Dorothy sets out for the Emerald City to get help from the Wonderful Wizard of Oz. Along the way, she meets a Scarecrow with no brain, a Tin Man with no heart, and a Cowardly Lion without courage. Together, they find the Wizard and ultimately conquer the Wicked Witch of the West, who has tried to thwart them at every turn. All acquire their heart's desire, and Dorothy and Toto find themselves safely back home in Kansas.

The Authors

Music and Lyrics by Harold Arlen and E.Y. Harburg; Background Music by Herbert Stothart; Adapted from the film by John Kane for the Royal Shakespeare Company (RSC). Based upon the Classical Motion Picture owned by Turner Entertainment Co. and distributed in all media by Warner Bros. Note: there is a second adaptation available for stage production with book adaptations by Frank Gabrielson. This version was originally produced by the Municipal Theatre of St. Louis (the MUNY) in 1945.

New York Run

There have been no Broadway or Off-Broadway productions of either the RSC or MUNY versions of this musical.

The Song
"If I Only Had a Brain"

Dorothy's first encounter on her journey to the Emerald City is with a Scarecrow perched in his cornfield. After she helps him down off of his pole, he bemoans the fact that he is unable to scare any of the crows away. He explains that he has no brain—only straw where his brain should be—and dreams of a better life in "If I Only Had a Brain." Note: in the RSC version, the Scarecrow is accompanied by a trio of singing crows.

Song Type
Standard Musical Theater/Tin Pan Alley Standard Uptempo

Suggested 16-Bar Cut for Auditions
m. 51 (including pick-up) to m. 67; sustain the vocal on "brain" and have the accompanist sustain beat 3 of m. 67 to finish.

PLOT SYNOPSES AND COMMENTARY BY
JOHN L. HAAG AND JEREMY MANN

The Songs

I'M NOT THAT SMART

(from "The 25th Annual Putnam County Spelling Bee")

Words and Music by
WILLIAM FINN

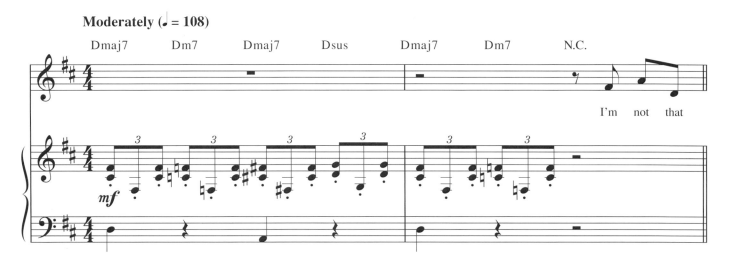
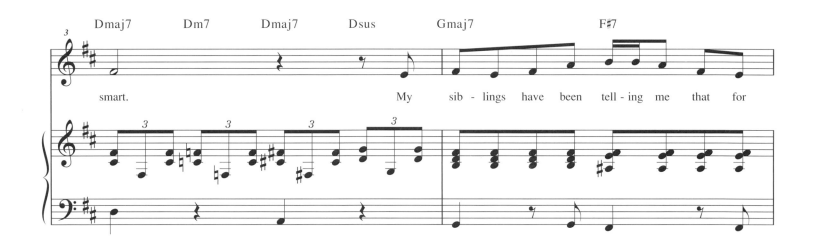
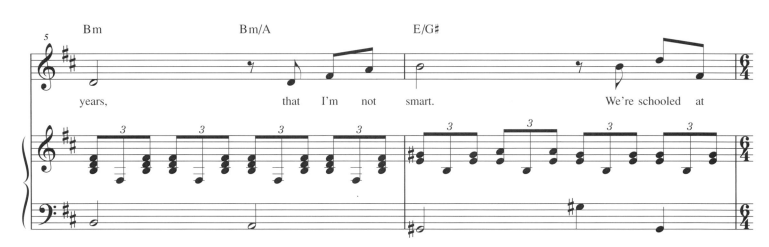

MY UNFORTUNATE ERECTION
(Chip's Lament)
(from "The 25th Annual Putnam County Spelling Bee")

Words and Music by
WILLIAM FINN

© 2005 WB MUSIC CORP. and IPSY PIPSY MUSIC
All Rights Administered by WB MUSIC CORP.
All Rights Reserved

DAMES
(from "42nd Street")

Words by
AL DUBIN

Music by
HARRY WARREN

RADAMES' LETTER
(from Elton John and Tim Rice's "Aida")

Lyrics by
TIM RICE

Music by
ELTON JOHN

Moderately slow

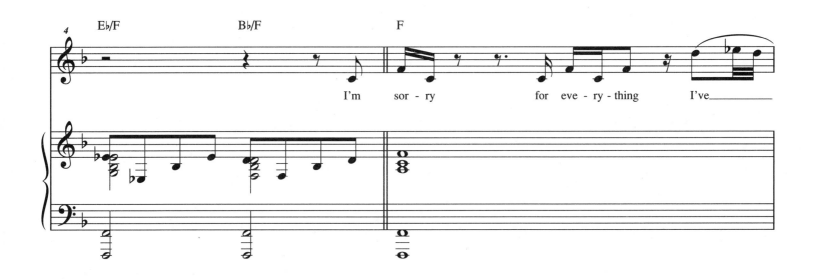

I'm sorry for everything I've

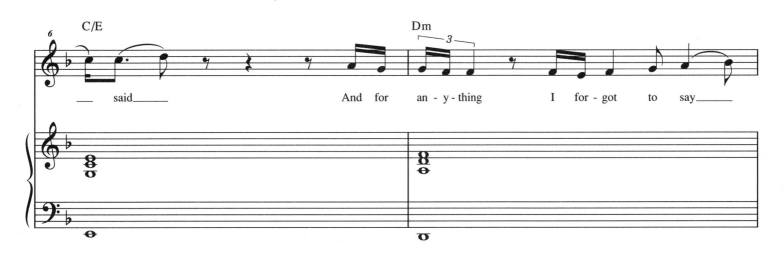

said And for anything I forgot to say

THE GYPSY IN ME
(from "Anything Goes—1987 Revival")

Words and Music by
COLE PORTER

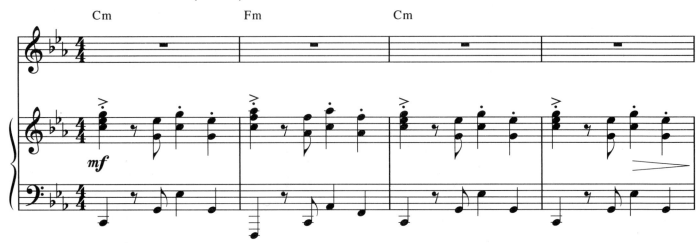

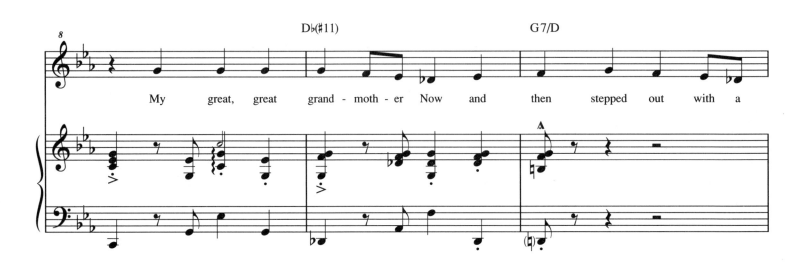

Long, long a-go, so long a-go I hard-ly know when, My great, great grand-moth-er Now and then stepped out with a

© 1934 (Renewed) WB MUSIC CORP.
All Rights Reserved

THE BALLAD OF BOOTH (PART III)
(from "Assassins")

Words and Music by
STEPHEN SONDHEIM

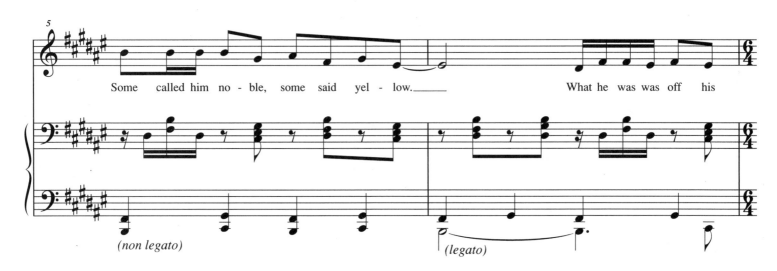

© 1990, 1992 RILTING MUSIC, INC.
All Rights Administered by WB MUSIC CORP.
All Rights Reserved

WHAT AM I DOIN'?
(from "Closer Than Ever")

Words by
RICHARD MALTBY, JR.

Music by
DAVID SHIRE

© 1984 PROGENY MUSIC, FIDDLEBACK MUSIC PUBLISHING CO., INC.,
LONG POND MUSIC and REVELATION MUSIC PUBLISHING CORP.
All Rights for PROGENY MUSIC and FIDDLEBACK MUSIC PUBLISHING CO., INC.
Administered by WARNER-TAMERLANE PUBLISHING CORP.
All Rights for LONG POND MUSIC and REVELATION MUSIC PUBLISHING CORP.
Administered by WB MUSIC CORP.
All Rights Reserved

BROADWAY BABY
(from "Dames At Sea")

Words by
GEORGE HAIMSOHN
and ROBIN MILLER

Music by
JIM WISE

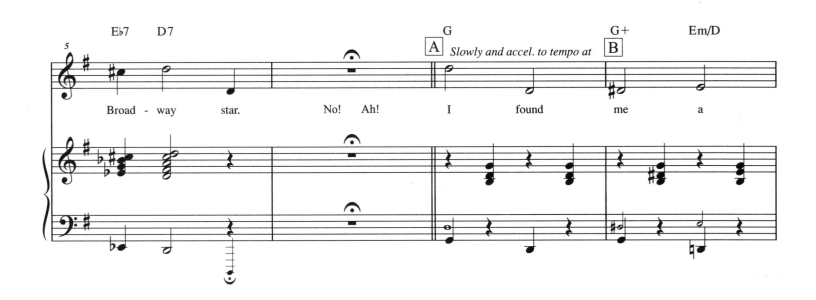

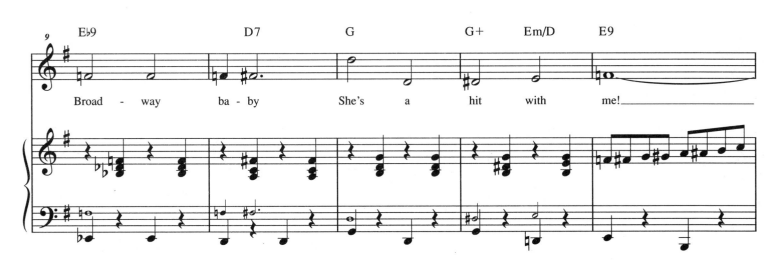

© 1966 (Renewed) EMI Hastings Catalog Inc.
All Rights Controlled by EMI Hastings Catalog Inc. (Publishing)
and ALFRED PUBLISHING CO., INC. (Print)
All Rights Reserved

BLAH, BLAH, BLAH
(from "Delicious")

Music and Lyrics by
GEORGE GERSHWIN and IRA GERSHWIN

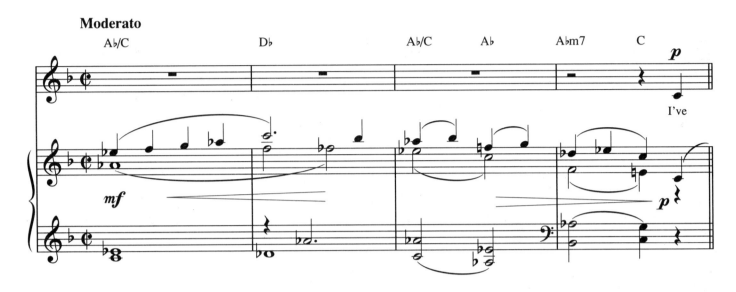

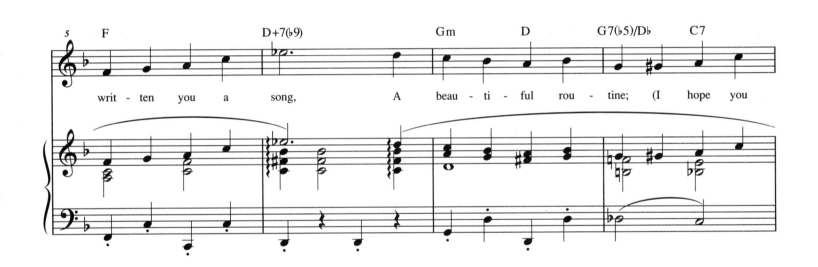

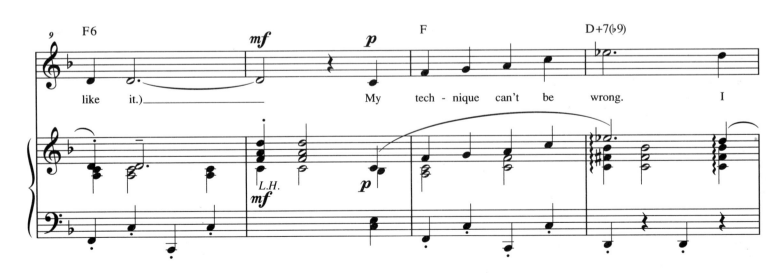

WHEN THE EARTH STOPPED TURNING
(from "Elegies")

Words and Music by
WILLIAM FINN

84

YOU GOTTA DIE SOMETIME
(from "Falsettos")

Words and Music by
WILLIAM FINN

I WANT TO MAKE MAGIC
(from "Fame-The Musical")

Lyrics by
STEVE MARGOSHES

Music by
JACQUES LEVY

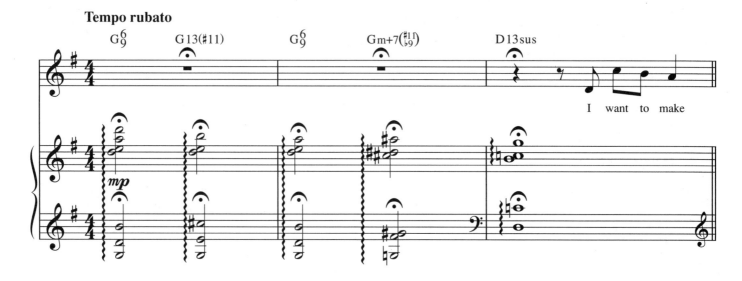
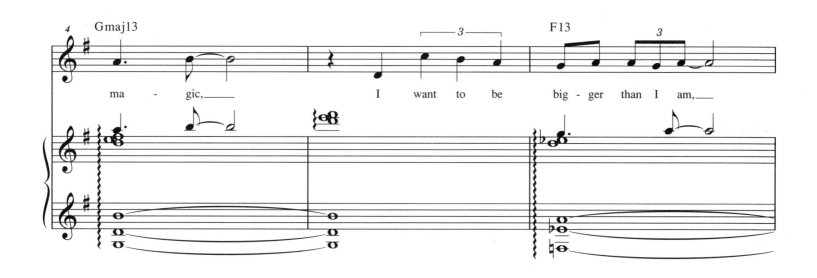
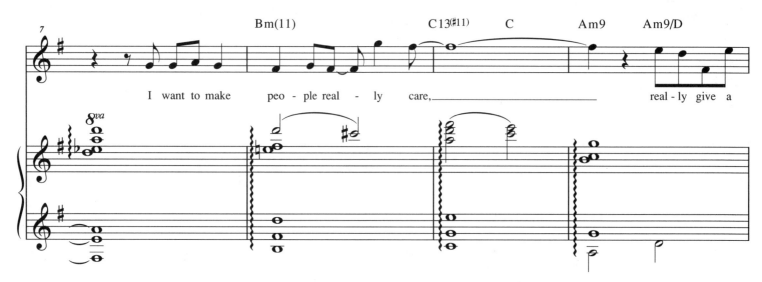

© 1986 WB MUSIC CORP., WARNER-TAMERLANE PUBLISHING CORP. and JACKELOPE PUBLISHING CO.
All Rights on behalf of itself and JACKELOPE PUBLISHING CO. Administered by
WARNER-TAMERLANE PUBLISHING CORP.
All Rights Reserved

SANDY
(from "Grease")

Words and Music by
LOUIS ST. LOUIS and SCOTT SIMON

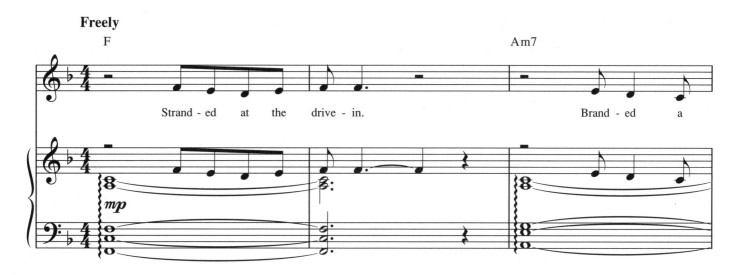

© 1978 ENSIGN MUSIC CORPORATION
All Rights Administered by UNICHAPPELL MUSIC INC.
All Rights Reserved

DIFFERENT
(from "Honk!")

Words by
ANTHONY DREWE

Music by
GEORGE STILES

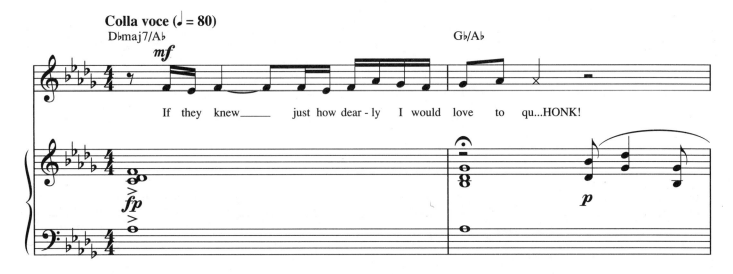
If they knew___ just how dear-ly I would love to qu...HONK!

But it's true___ I'm a bird who seems to lack the knack

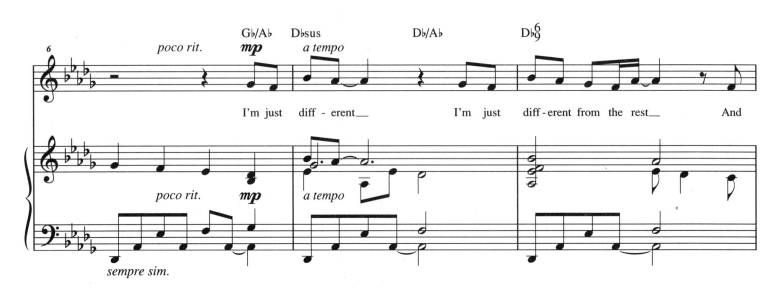
I'm just diff-erent___ I'm just diff-erent from the rest___ And

KNOWING ME, KNOWING YOU
(from "Mamma Mia")

Words and Music by BENNY ANDERSSON,
STIG ANDERSON and BJORN ULVAEUS

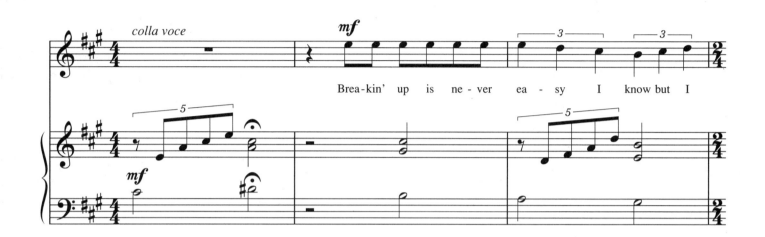

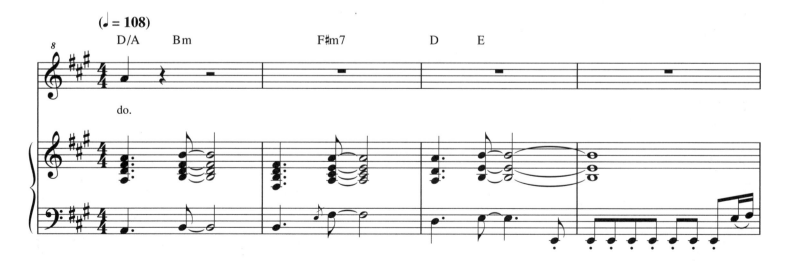

TO EACH HIS DULCINEA
(To Every Man His Dream)
(from "The Man Of La Mancha")

Words by
JOE DARION

Music by
MITCH LEIGH

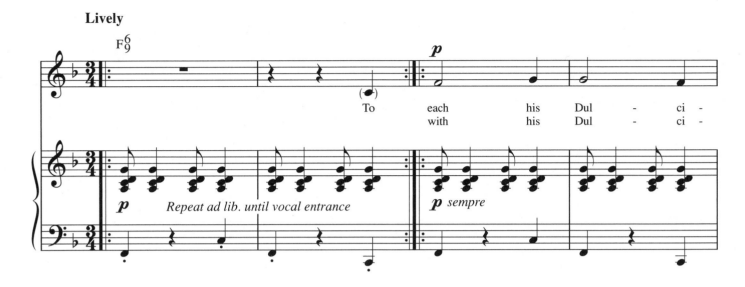

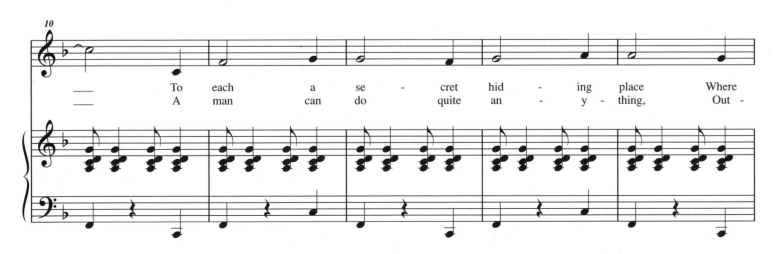

© 1965 (Renewed) HELENA MUSIC COMPANY and ANDREW SCOTT MUSIC
All Rights in the U.S. and Canada Administered by CHERRY LANE MUSIC PUBLISHING COMPANY
All Rights Reserved   Used by Permission

I'M FALLING IN LOVE WITH SOMEONE
(from "Naughty Marrietta")

Lyrics by
RIDA JOHNSON YOUNG

Music by
VICTOR HERBERT

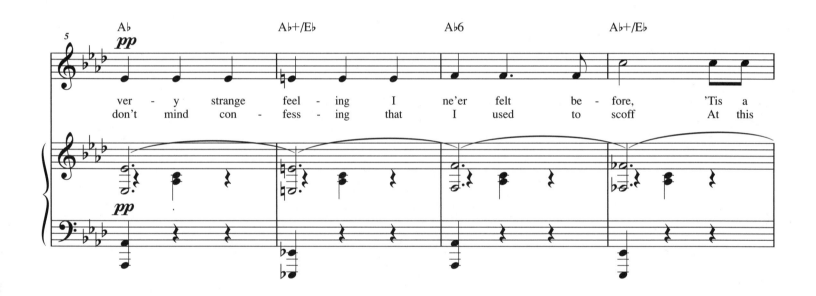

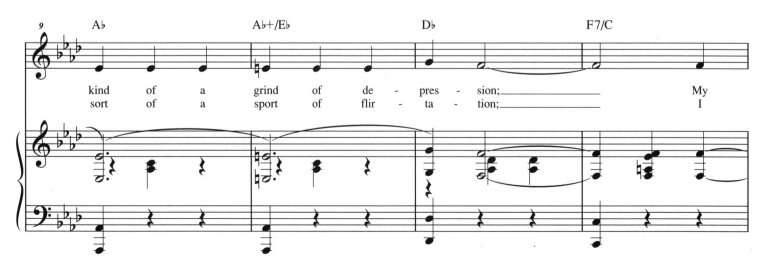

I'm Falling In Love With Someone - 4 - 1
29008

© 2007 ALFRED PUBLISHING CO., INC.
All Rights Reserved

AND THEY'RE OFF
(from "A New Brain")

Words and Music by
WILLIAM FINN

© 1998 WB MUSIC CORP. and IPSY PIPSY MUSIC
All Rights Administered by WB MUSIC CORP.
All Rights Reserved

150

STOUTHEARTED MEN
(from "The New Moon")

Lyrics by
OSCAR HAMMERSTEIN II

Music by
SIGMUND ROMBERG

Tempo di Marcia

Give me some men who are stout-heart-ed men, Who will

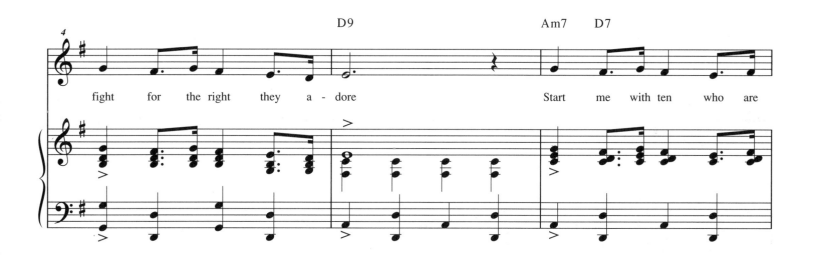

fight for the right they a-dore Start me with ten who are

stout-heart-ed men And I'll soon give you ten thou-sand more. Oh,

© 1927 (Renewed) WARNER BROS. INC.
Rights for the Extended Term of Copyright in the U.S. Controlled by
WB MUSIC CORP. and BAMBALINA MUSIC
All Rights Reserved

LUCKY TO BE ME
(from "On The Town")

Lyrics by
BETTY COMDEN and ADOLPH GREEN

Music by
LEONARD BERNSTEIN

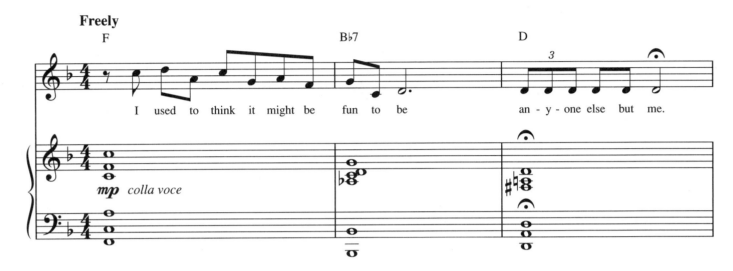

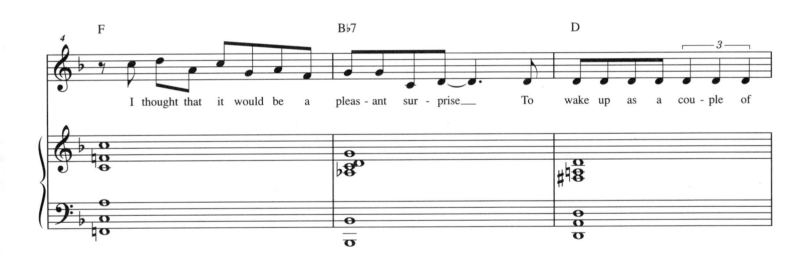

A NEW TOWN IS A BLUE TOWN
(from "The Pajama Game")

Words and Music by
RICHARD ADLER and JERRY ROSS

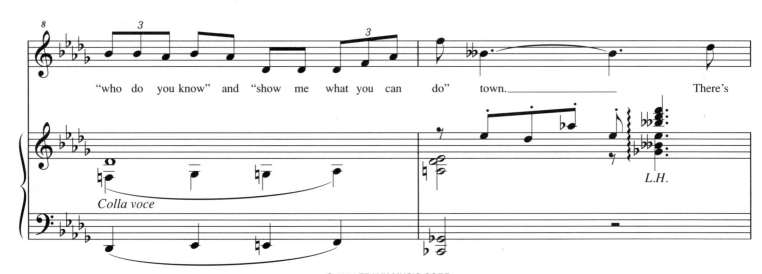

© 1954 FRANK MUSIC CORP.
© Renewed and Assigned to J & J ROSS CO. and LAKSHMI PUJA MUSIC LTD.
All Rights Administered by THE SONGWRITERS GUILD OF AMERICA
All Rights Reserved

THERE'S A BOAT DAT'S LEAVIN' SOON FOR NEW YORK
(from "Porgy And Bess")

Music and Lyrics by GEORGE GERSHWIN, DU BOSE and DOROTHY HEYWARD and IRA GERSHWIN

YOU TOOK ADVANTAGE OF ME

(from "Present Arms")

Words by
LORENZ HART

Music by
RICHARD RODGERS

In the spring when the feel-ing was chron-ic____ and my

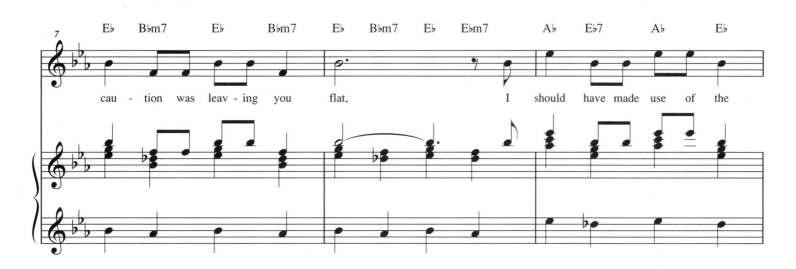

cau-tion was leav-ing you flat, I should have made use of the

© 1928 (Renewed) WARNER BROS.INC.
All Rights for the Extended Renewal Term in the U.S. Controlled by
WB MUSIC CORP. and WILLIAMSON MUSIC CO.
All Rights Reserved

188

ALONE IN THE UNIVERSE
(from "Seussical the Musical")

Lyrics by
LYNN AHRENS

Music by
STEPHEN FLAHERTY

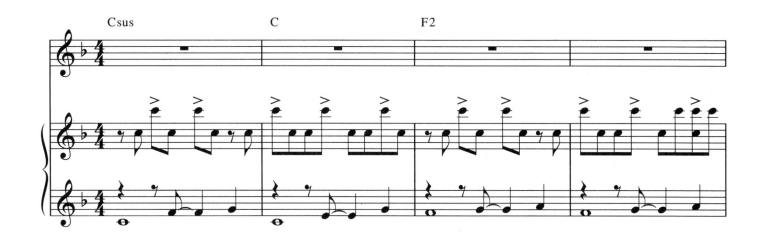

I'm a-lone in the u-ni-verse. So a-lone in the u-ni-verse.

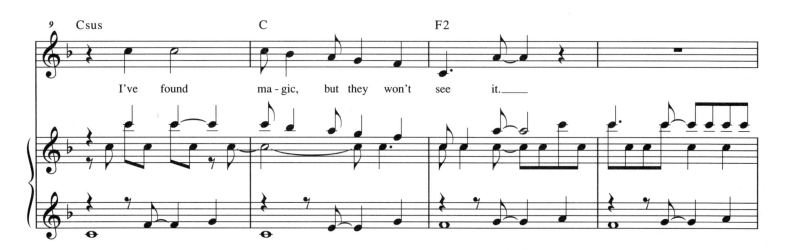

I've found ma-gic, but they won't see it.

© 2001 WB MUSIC CORP., PEN AND PERSEVERANCE and HILLSDALE MUSIC, INC.
All Rights Administered by WB MUSIC CORP.
All Rights Reserved

Something to Live For

(from "Sophisticated Ladies")

Words and Music by
DUKE ELLINGTON and BILLY STRAYHORN

STRIKE UP THE BAND
(from "Strike Up The Band")

Music and Lyrics by
GEORGE GERSHWIN and IRA GERSHWIN

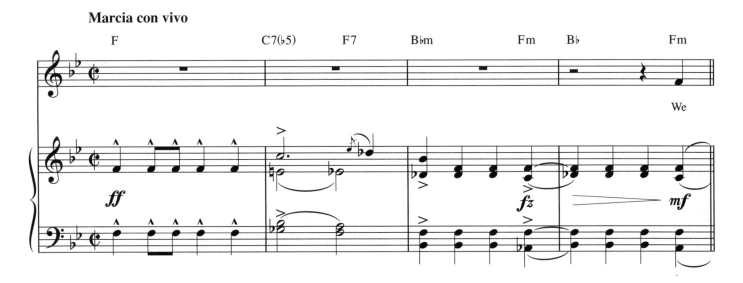

© 1927 (Renewed) WB MUSIC CORP.
GERSHWIN® and GEORGE GERSHWIN® are registered trademarks of Gershwin Enterprises
IRA GERSHWIN™ is a trademark of Gershwin Enterprises
All Rights Reserved

Ballad Of The Easy Life
(from "The Threepenny Opera")

English Words by
MARC BLITZSTEIN
Original German Words by
BERTOLT BRECHT

Music by
KURT WEILL

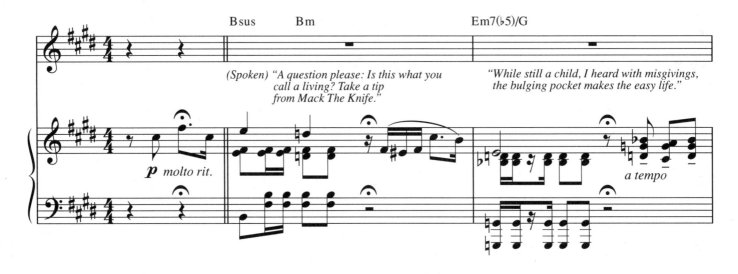

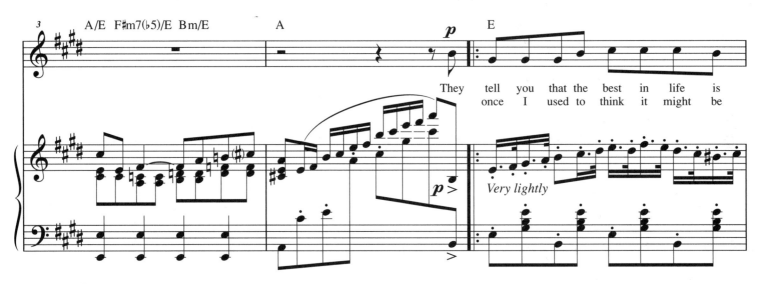

© 1928 UNIVERSAL EDITION
© 1955 WEILL-BRECHT-HARMS CO., INC.
Renewal Rights Assigned to the ESTATE OF MARC BLITZSTEIN, BERT BRECHT
and KURT WEILL FOUNDATION FOR MUSIC
All Rights Administered by WB MUSIC CORP.
All Rights Reserved

LOVE'S REVENGE
(from "Two Gentlemen Of Verona")

Lyrics by
JOHN GUARE

Music by
GALT MacDERMOT

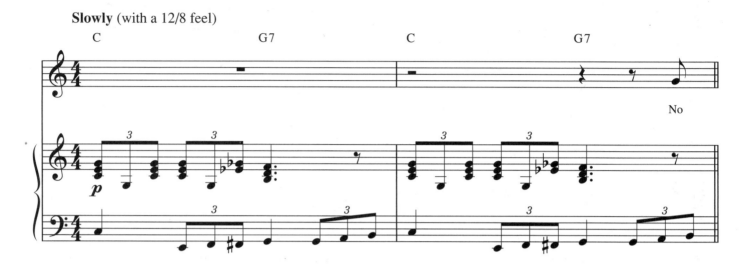

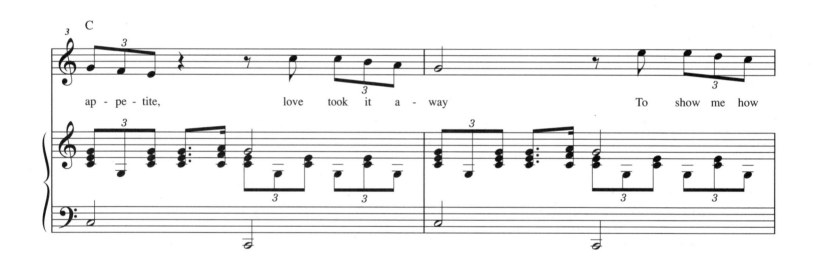

© 1971, 1972 (Copyrights Renewed) by GALT MacDERMOT and JOHN GUARE
Publication and Allied Rights Assigned to CHAPPELL & CO., INC.
All Rights Reserved

THEY WON'T KNOW ME
(from "Wish You Were Here")

Words and Music by
HAROLD ROME

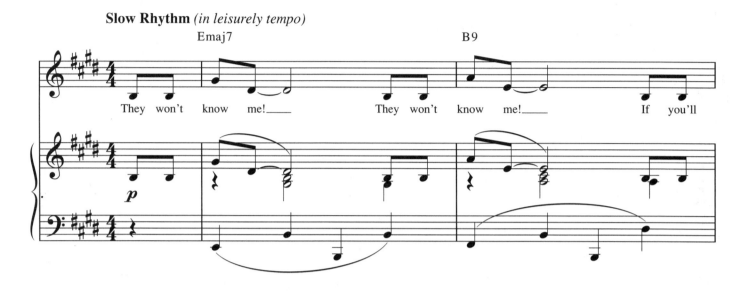
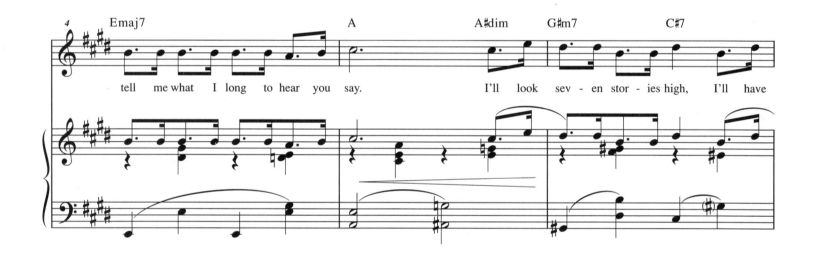
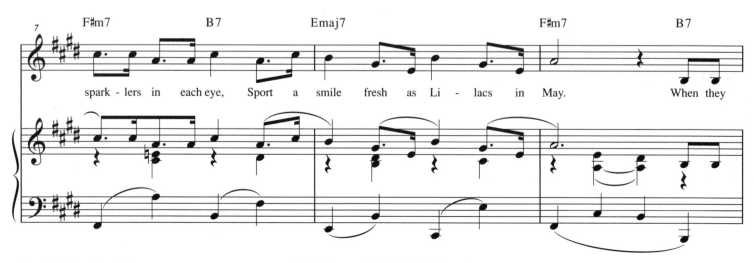

IF I ONLY HAD A BRAIN
(from "The Wizard Of Oz")

Lyrics by
E. Y. HARBURG

Music by
HAROLD ARLEN

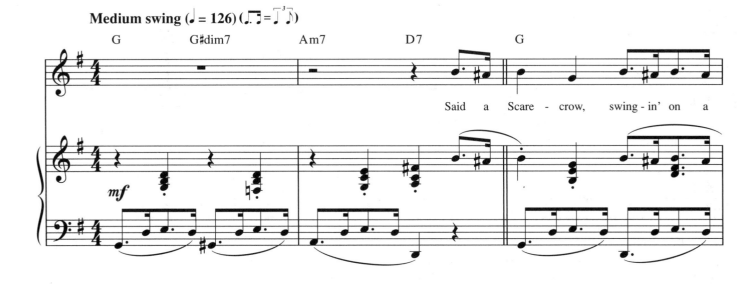

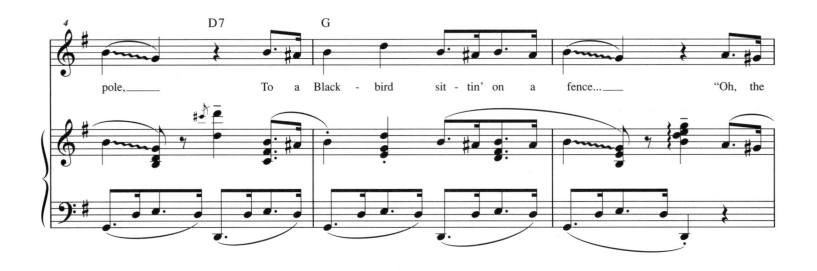

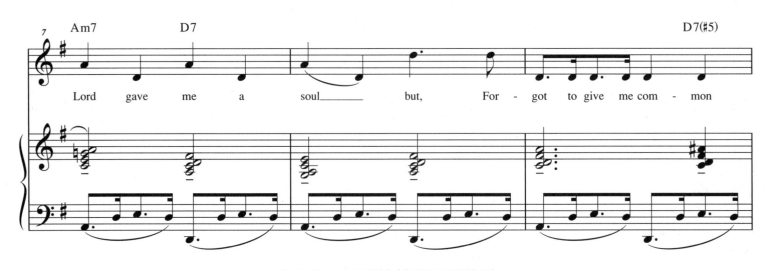

© 1938 (Renewed) METRO-GOLDWYN-MAYER INC.
© 1939 (Renewed) EMI FEIST CATALOG INC.
Rights throughout the World Controlled by EMI FEIST CATALOG INC. (Publishing)
and ALFRED PUBLISHING CO., INC. (Print)
All Rights Reserved